CHOOSING YOUR CAREER PATH

The Handbook for College Students and High Schoolers

Choosing Your Career Path Being an Introvert or Extrovert, Zodiac Sign and DNA

Dr. Lester G. Reid

The Author of the #1 Amazon Hot New Release, "Problem-Based Learning: The Hand Book for Instructors and Scholars."

COPYRIGHT

ACKNOWLEDGEMENT

Writing a book is a transformative journey that would not be possible without the support and contributions of numerous individuals. As I bring my book, "Choosing Your Career Path: The Handbook for College Students and High Schoolers," to completion, I would like to express my heartfelt appreciation to those who have played a significant role in its creation.

First and foremost, I am deeply grateful to the college students and high schoolers who inspired me to undertake this project. Your unwavering determination, curiosity, and thirst for knowledge have been the driving force behind every page I have written. It is your desire to navigate the complexities of career choices and forge a path to a fulfilling future that has fueled my dedication to creating this handbook.

I extend my sincere gratitude to the educators, career counselors, and professionals who have generously shared their expertise and insights with me. Your guidance, wisdom, and unwavering support have been invaluable in shaping the content of this handbook. Your dedication to empowering young minds and equipping them with the necessary tools for making informed career decisions is commendable.

To the parents and guardians who have selflessly supported and encouraged their children's educational journeys, I express my deepest appreciation. Your unwavering belief in the power of education and the importance of making informed career choices has been instrumental in the development of this handbook. Your tireless efforts to nurture and guide young minds inspire me.

I also acknowledge the countless researchers, authors, and experts whose work and insights have influenced the content of this handbook. Your contributions to the field of career development have paved the way for a comprehensive and impactful guide, ensuring its accuracy, relevance, and usefulness.

Finally, I want to express my heartfelt appreciation to the readers of this handbook. It is your interest, enthusiasm, and thirst for knowledge that make the creation of this book worthwhile. I hope that "Choosing Your Career Path: The Handbook for College Students and High Schoolers" serves as a valuable companion on your journey toward discovering your passions, making informed decisions, and building a successful and fulfilling career.

I acknowledge the collective effort and support that have gone into the creation of this handbook. Each person mentioned and many others who have contributed in their own unique ways have played an instrumental role in shaping this resource, and I am deeply grateful for their involvement. May "Choosing Your Career Path: The Handbook for College Students and High Schoolers" serve as a guiding light for aspiring individuals seeking to navigate the world of career choices and unlock their full potential.

Table of Contents

ABOUT THIS BOOK

Choosing a career path is one of the most important decisions we make in our lives. It shapes not only our professional trajectory but also our overall happiness and fulfillment. For college students and high schoolers, the task of choosing a career can be both exciting and daunting. With countless options available and a multitude of factors to consider, it's essential to have a reliable guide to navigate this crucial phase of life.

"Choosing Your Career Path: The Handbook for College Students and High Schoolers" is a comprehensive resource designed to assist individuals in making informed decisions about their future. This handbook aims to empower readers by providing them with valuable insights, practical advice, and tools to explore their passions, skills, and aspirations. The journey of selecting a career path is not a one-size-fits-all approach. Each individual possesses unique talents, interests, and personality traits that influence their professional choices. This handbook recognizes the importance of aligning one's career with their intrinsic qualities, ensuring a fulfilling and meaningful career journey.

Throughout the pages of this handbook, readers will examine various aspects of career exploration and decision-making. From understanding personal strengths and interests to exploring different industries and professions, each chapter offers valuable guidance and exercises to facilitate self-reflection and discovery. The handbook also emphasizes the significance of research and exploration. It provides valuable resources to gather information about different career paths, including educational requirements, job prospects, and potential earnings.

Furthermore, this handbook recognizes the dynamic nature of the modern job market. It sheds light on emerging industries and professions, highlighting the importance of adaptability and continuous learning in navigating an ever-evolving professional landscape. It encourages readers to embrace a growth mindset and seize opportunities for personal and professional development.

Furthermore, to individual self-assessment and career exploration, this handbook also addresses practical aspects of career preparation, such as resume writing, interview skills, and networking strategies. It equips readers with the necessary tools to present themselves effectively to potential employers and make a lasting impression in a competitive job market. "Choosing Your Career Path: The Handbook for College Students and High Schoolers" is not just a manual but a companion on the journey of self-discovery and career exploration. It is a trusted resource that seeks to empower individuals to make informed decisions, pursue their passions, and achieve success and fulfillment in their chosen careers.

So, whether you're a college student embarking on your academic journey or a high schooler contemplating your future, this handbook is here to guide you, inspire you, and provide you with the knowledge and confidence to choose a career path that aligns with who you are and what you aspire to become. Let the journey begin!

PREFACE

In the vast landscape of career possibilities, finding the right path can be an overwhelming endeavor. Many factors come into play when making such a significant decision, and understanding ourselves is paramount. In this preface, we embark on a fascinating exploration of the interplay between personality traits, astrological influences, and genetic predispositions in the context of choosing a career path.

The dichotomy of introversion and extroversion has long fascinated psychologists and individuals alike. Introverts derive energy from within, seeking solace in solitary environments, while extroverts thrive on social interactions and external stimuli. By examining these fundamental aspects of personality, we shed light on the types of work environments, job roles, and career paths that best suit introverted and extroverted individuals.

Beyond personality traits, astrology offers another lens through which we can gain insights into ourselves and our career preferences. Each zodiac sign represents unique characteristics, strengths, and weaknesses. By examine the connection between zodiac signs and career choices, we unlock hidden potentials, uncover compatibility with certain professions, and find inspiration in aligning our path with the cosmic energies of the universe.

Moreover, our genetic makeup, encoded in our DNA, influences various aspects of our lives, including our cognitive abilities, skills, and talents. Understanding our genetic predispositions provides invaluable insights into our strengths and weaknesses, allowing us to make more informed decisions about the career paths that are most likely to lead to fulfillment and success.

By weaving together, the threads of introversion and extroversion, astrology, and genetics, we create a tapestry of self-discovery and personal growth. This multidimensional approach empowers individuals to navigate their career paths with confidence and authenticity. It encourages us to reflect on our natural inclinations, embrace our unique qualities, and align our choices with the essence of who we are.

However, it is crucial to recognize that personality traits, astrology, and genetics are not sole determinants of our career paths. They serve as valuable tools for self-reflection and exploration, but they do not dictate our choices. Each individual is a complex blend of various influences, experiences, and aspirations. Ultimately, our career decisions should reflect a combination of self-awareness, practical considerations, and personal values.

Together, we embark on a journey of self-discovery, guided by the exploration of introversion and extroversion, astrology, and genetics in the context of choosing a career path. We present a collection of insights, research, and practical advice to help readers navigate this complex terrain. Through thought-provoking discussions, real-life examples, and actionable steps, we aim to empower individuals to make informed choices, find purpose and fulfillment, and embark on a career path that resonates with their authentic selves.

We encourage readers to approach this book with an open mind and a willingness to examine their own unique qualities. Each chapter offers an opportunity for self-reflection and self-discovery. It is our hope that the knowledge, wisdom, and guidance shared within these pages will serve as a compass, illuminating the path toward a fulfilling and meaningful career.

As you embark on this journey, remember that choosing your career path is a deeply personal and transformative process. May this exploration of introversion, extroversion, astrology, and genetics inspire you, spark introspection, and empower you to make choices that align with your true self.

CHAPTER ONE

Choosing Your Career Path

Choosing a career path is one of the most important decisions we make in our lives. It determines our professional growth, financial stability, and overall satisfaction. However, navigating the complex world of career choices can be overwhelming. To help you make informed decisions, this book presents a comprehensive guide on the do's and don'ts of choosing your career path. By following these guidelines, you can increase your chances of finding a fulfilling and successful career. Deciding a career path is a significant decision that can shape the course of our lives. It is a process that involves introspection, research, and careful consideration. A well-chosen career path can lead to personal fulfillment, professional growth, and a sense of purpose. This book explores the importance of choosing a career path, the factors to consider, and the steps to take in making an informed decision.

Choosing a career path is crucial for several reasons. Firstly, it determines the direction of our professional lives and the opportunities we pursue. A well-aligned career path allows us to utilize our skills, interests, and passions, enhancing our motivation and job satisfaction. Secondly, a chosen career path can provide financial stability and security, enabling us to meet our personal and financial goals. Additionally, a fulfilling career can positively impact our overall well-being, as we spend a significant portion of our lives at work. When we engage in meaningful work, it enhances our sense of purpose, boosts our self-esteem, and contributes to a balanced and fulfilling life.

The Do's:

1. **Self-Reflection:** Before embarking on your career journey, take the time for self-reflection. Assess your interests, values, strengths, and weaknesses. Consider what you enjoy doing and what motivates you. Understanding yourself will provide clarity and enable you to align your career choices with your passions and skills.

2. **Research:** Thoroughly research different career options that align with your interests. Gather information about job prospects, salary ranges, educational requirements, and industry trends. Use online resources, attend career fairs, and network with professionals to gain insights into various fields. Research helps you make informed decisions and prevents surprises down the road.

3. **Seek Guidance:** Seek guidance from professionals, mentors, and career counselors. They can provide valuable advice, share their experiences, and offer insights into different industries. A mentor can provide guidance and support, helping

you navigate the challenges of your chosen career path. Collaborating with knowledgeable individuals can help you make well-informed decisions.

4. **Gain Practical Experience**: Internships, part-time jobs, and volunteer work can provide invaluable practical experience. Seek opportunities to gain hands-on experience in your field of interest. Practical exposure allows you to assess if a particular career path is the right fit for you. Additionally, it enhances your resume and gives you a competitive edge in the job market.

5. **Continuous Learning:** In today's dynamic work environment, it is essential to embrace lifelong learning. Stay updated with industry trends, technological advancements, and new skills required in your chosen field. Attend workshops, conferences, and seminars to enhance your knowledge and skills. Continuous learning ensures that you remain relevant and adaptable in a rapidly evolving job market.

6. **Network:** Build a strong professional network by attending industry events, joining relevant associations, and leveraging social media platforms like LinkedIn. Networking opens doors to new opportunities, exposes you to different perspectives, and allows you to learn from experienced professionals.

Cultivating meaningful connections can lead to mentorship, job referrals, and collaborations.

7. **Set Realistic Goals**: Set realistic and achievable short-term and long-term goals. Break down your career aspirations into actionable steps. By setting goals, you can track your progress, stay motivated, and make strategic decisions aligned with your objectives. However, it is essential to remain flexible and adapt your goals as you gain new insights and experiences.

The Don'ts:

1. **Following Others' Expectations:** Avoid choosing a career path solely based on others' expectations, whether it be your parents, friends, or societal pressure. While it is important to consider advice from trusted individuals, ultimately, you should make decisions based on your own interests and aspirations. Pursuing a career that aligns with your passion and values will bring greater satisfaction and fulfillment.

2. **Rushing the Decision:** Choosing a career path is a significant decision that requires thoughtful consideration. Avoid rushing into a decision without proper research and self-reflection. Take the time to explore different options, gain insights, and evaluate potential

career paths. Patience and thoroughness in decision-making will lead to better outcomes in the long run.

3. **Neglecting Work-Life Balance:** When choosing a career path, consider the work-life balance it offers. A fulfilling career should not come at the expense of your personal life, relationships, or well-being. Ensure that the demands and expectations of your chosen career align with your desired lifestyle. Seek a career that allows you to maintain a healthy balance between work and personal life.

4. **Fear of Change:** Don't let the fear of change hold you back from exploring new career opportunities. The job market evolves, and your interests and goals may change over time. Embrace new challenges, be open to learning, and consider making career switches if necessary. It's never too late to pursue a different path that aligns better with your aspirations.

5. **Neglecting Financial Considerations:** While passion and fulfillment are crucial, financial considerations cannot be ignored. Assess the earning potential of your chosen career path, taking into account factors such as salary growth, job stability, and market demand. Consider your financial obligations and lifestyle preferences to ensure your

chosen career provides the necessary financial stability.

6. **Overlooking Transferable Skills:** When evaluating career options, don't overlook the value of transferable skills. These skills, such as communication, problem-solving, and leadership abilities, can be applied across various industries and roles. Identify your transferable skills and consider how they can be leveraged in different career paths. This widens your options and increases your adaptability.

7. **Settling for Mediocrity:** Avoid settling for a career that does not excite or challenge you. Aim for a career that ignites your passion and allows you to grow both personally and professionally. Strive for excellence, and don't be afraid to pursue ambitious goals. By seeking a career that aligns with your true potential, you increase the likelihood of long-term success and fulfillment.

Choosing a career path is a significant decision that requires careful consideration and self-reflection. By following the do's and avoiding the don'ts outlined in this guide, you can increase your chances of finding a fulfilling and successful career. Remember, your career journey is unique, and it may evolve over time. Embrace new opportunities, stay adaptable, and never stop pursuing your passions and aspirations. With the right mindset and approach, you can build a rewarding career that aligns with your values and brings you long-term happiness.

Choosing a career path is a significant decision that influences our professional and personal lives. By considering factors such as interests, skills, values, and market demand, we can make an informed decision. Engaging in self-assessment, research, exploration, seeking guidance, setting goals, and embracing flexibility are essential steps in this process. A well-chosen career path leads to personal fulfillment, professional growth, and a sense of purpose, enabling us to create a successful and satisfying career journey.

The BEST Career Path

Choosing the best career path is a decision that can significantly impact our lives, shaping our personal fulfillment, financial stability, and overall well-being. However, with countless career options available, it can be challenging to identify the path that aligns with our interests, skills, and aspirations. Together, we will examine the process of choosing the best career path by examining various factors, including personal attributes, market trends, and future prospects. By adopting a personal and strategic approach, you can navigate the career landscape with confidence and increase your chances of finding a fulfilling and successful career.

1. Understanding Your Interests, Passions, and Values The first step in choosing the best

career path is self-assessment. Take the time to reflect on your interests, passions, and values. What subjects or activities excite you? What causes or issues are important to you? Identifying your passions and aligning them with potential career options can provide a strong foundation for making informed choices.

2. Identifying Strengths and Skills Recognizing your strengths and skills is crucial when determining the best career path for you. Assess your natural abilities, talents, and acquired skills. Consider areas where you excel and tasks that come to you effortlessly. Identifying your strengths allows you to leverage them in a career that aligns with your abilities and maximizes your potential for success.

3. Researching and Exploring Career Options To choose the best career path, it is essential to conduct thorough research and explore various options. Look into different industries, job roles, and career paths that align with your interests and strengths. Consider factors such as job prospects, growth opportunities, work-life balance, and alignment with your long-term goals. Utilize online resources, informational interviews, and networking to gather insights and gain a deeper understanding of different career paths.

4. Market Trends and Future Prospects Understanding market trends and future prospects is vital when choosing a career path. Consider industries that are experiencing growth, technological advancements, and emerging fields. Stay informed about changing market demands and the skills that are in high demand. By aligning your career choice with market trends, you increase the likelihood of finding job security and growth opportunities in the future.

5. Seeking Guidance: Mentors and Career Counselors Seeking guidance from mentors and career counselors can provide valuable insights and support in your career exploration. Experienced professionals can offer guidance based on their own experiences and provide industry-specific knowledge. Career counselors can administer assessments and provide guidance based on your strengths, interests, and goals. Their expertise can assist you in narrowing down your options and making informed decisions.

6. Gaining Hands-on Experience: Internships and Volunteering Gaining hands-on experience through internships, volunteering, or part-time work is invaluable when choosing a career path. This practical exposure allows you to test the waters, gain

insight into the day-to-day realities of different professions, and evaluate whether they align with your expectations and interests. It also provides an opportunity to build a network, develop new skills, and enhance your resume.

7. Balancing Passion and Practicality When choosing the best career path, it is essential to strike a balance between passion and practicality. While it's important to pursue work that aligns with your interests and passions, practical considerations such as financial stability, job prospects, and market demand should also be taken into account. Evaluate your financial obligations, lifestyle goals, and the feasibility of pursuing your chosen career path.

8. Continuous Learning and Adaptability Choosing the best career path is not a one-time decision but an ongoing process. Industries evolve, technologies advance, and new opportunities arise. Therefore, it is crucial to embrace continuous learning and develop adaptability. Commit to staying updated with industry trends, acquiring new skills, and being open to change. A willingness to learn and adapt ensures that your career remains relevant and provides opportunities for growth.

9. Networking and Building Connections Building a strong professional network is essential for career development. Attend industry events, join professional organizations, and connect with like-minded individuals in your desired field. Networking can lead to valuable opportunities, mentorship, and a deeper understanding of your chosen industry. Nurture relationships, seek advice, and leverage connections to expand your career options.

10. Evaluating Personal Fulfillment and Long-Term Goals Ultimately, choosing the best career path should be driven by personal fulfillment and alignment with your long-term goals. Consider the potential for growth, the impact you can make, and the level of satisfaction a career choice can provide. Assess how a particular career aligns with your personal values, work-life balance preferences, and overall life goals. Strive to find a career that not only brings financial stability but also brings a sense of purpose and fulfillment.

Choosing the best career path requires a thoughtful and strategic approach. By conducting self-assessment, exploring various career options, considering market trends, seeking guidance, gaining practical experience, and balancing passion with practicality, you can increase your chances of making an informed decision. Remember to continuously learn, adapt, and evaluate personal fulfillment and long-term goals. With dedication, self-reflection, and a proactive mindset, you can embark on a career path that brings fulfillment, success, and personal satisfaction.

Choosing the best career path is a significant decision that influences our professional and personal lives. By considering factors such as interests, skills, values, personality fit, and industry trends, we can make an informed decision. Engaging in self-reflection, thorough research, networking, skill development, and seeking guidance are crucial steps in this process. The best career path is one that aligns with our passions, utilizes our strengths, and provides opportunities for growth and fulfillment. By navigating the career selection process with diligence and self-awareness, we can embark on a journey that leads to personal success and satisfaction.

Do What You Are Cut Out to Do

Choosing a career path is a significant decision that can shape the course of our lives. However, many individuals feel compelled to pursue careers based on external expectations, societal norms, or financial considerations rather than considering their true passions and abilities. Together, we will explore the importance of choosing a career path that aligns with your natural inclinations and talents. By focusing on what you're cut out for, rather than what you think you must do, you can pave the way for a fulfilling and successful professional journey.

1. **Self-Discovery:** Understanding Your Interests and Passions The first step in choosing a career that suits you is self-discovery. Take the time to explore your interests, passions, and values. Reflect on activities that bring you joy, engage your curiosity, and give you a sense of fulfillment. By understanding your own inclinations and desires, you can identify career paths that align with your personal interests.

2. **Identifying Your Strengths and Abilities:** Knowing your strengths and abilities is crucial in finding a career that you're cut out for. Assess your natural talents, skills, and aptitudes. Consider the areas where you excel and the tasks that come to you effortlessly. By leveraging your strengths, you can find a career that allows you to perform at your best and make a meaningful impact.

3. **Assessing Personality Traits and Work:** Style Personality traits and work style play a significant role in determining job satisfaction and success. Consider whether you are an introvert or an extrovert, and how this impacts your energy levels and preferred work environments. Reflect on whether you thrive in structured or flexible settings, prefer teamwork or individual work, and whether

you enjoy taking risks or prefer stability. Understanding these aspects can help you find a career path that suits your personality and work preferences.

4. **Exploring Career Options:** Research and Information Gathering Once you have a clear understanding of your interests, strengths, and personality, start exploring different career options. Conduct thorough research and gather information about various industries, job roles, and growth opportunities. Use online resources, informational interviews, and job shadowing to gain insights into different professions. Consider the educational requirements, job prospects, work-life balance, and potential for growth in each field.

5. **Seeking Guidance:** Mentors and Career Counselors Seeking guidance from mentors and career counselors can provide valuable insights and support in your career exploration journey. Experienced professionals can offer firsthand knowledge about specific industries and provide advice based on their own experiences. Career counselors can administer aptitude and personality tests to help you gain a deeper understanding of your strengths and interests. Their guidance can assist you in narrowing down your career choices and making informed decisions.

6. **Experimenting and Gaining Experience:** Hands-on experience is invaluable in determining whether a career is the right fit for you. Seek opportunities to intern, volunteer, or work part-time in fields that interest you. This firsthand experience will give you a glimpse into the day-to-day realities of different professions and help you evaluate whether they align with your expectations and preferences.

7. **Embracing Flexibility and Adaptability:** As you navigate your career path, it's important to remain flexible and open to new opportunities. Your interests and goals may evolve over time, and being adaptable allows you to explore different paths and make necessary adjustments. Embracing change and being willing to step outside your comfort zone can lead to unexpected and fulfilling career opportunities.

8. **Continuous Learning and Professional:** Development Once you have chosen a career path that aligns with your interests and abilities, commit to continuous learning and professional development. Stay updated with industry trends, acquire new skills, and seek out growth opportunities. Continuous learning not only enhances your expertise but also keeps you motivated and engaged in your chosen field.

9. **Balancing Passion and Practicality:** While following your passion is important, it is essential to strike a balance between passion and practicality. Consider the financial aspects of your chosen career, such as earning potential, job stability, and the cost of education or training. Assess your financial obligations and lifestyle goals to ensure that your career choice provides the necessary stability and support for your desired lifestyle.

10. **Embracing Your Unique Journey:** Remember that your career journey is unique to you. Avoid comparing yourself to others or succumbing to societal expectations. Embrace the path that feels right for you, even if it diverges from the norm. Trust your instincts, stay true to your values, and have confidence in your abilities. Your career should reflect who you are and bring you a sense of fulfillment and purpose.

Choosing a career path that aligns with your natural inclinations and abilities is essential for long-term satisfaction and success. By focusing on what you're cut out for, rather than what you think you must do, you can create a fulfilling professional journey. Invest time in self-discovery, assess your strengths and interests, consider your personality traits and work style, and gather information about various career options. Seek guidance from mentors and career counselors, gain hands-on experience, and remain flexible and open to new opportunities. Remember to strike a balance between passion and practicality, and continuously invest in your professional development. Ultimately, embrace your unique journey and trust that choosing a career path based on who you are will lead you to a fulfilling and rewarding future.

The Distinction Between a Career and a Job

In everyday language, the terms "career" and "job" are often used interchangeably. However, they represent two distinct concepts In the field of work. Understanding the difference between a career and a job is crucial for individuals seeking long-term professional fulfillment and growth. Together, we will explore the definitions of a career and a job, examine their key differences, and discuss the implications of each in terms of personal development and satisfaction.

1. **Defining a Career:** A career is a long-term, progressive professional journey encompassing a series of related jobs and experiences. It involves personal growth, skill development, and the pursuit of professional goals and aspirations. A career is characterized by a sense of purpose, a strategic approach to professional advancement, and a commitment to continuous learning and development. It often involves building expertise, assuming

increasing levels of responsibility, and making deliberate choices aligned with one's passions and values.

2. **Understanding a Job:** A job, on the other hand, is a specific, finite employment position with defined tasks and responsibilities. It is typically focused on the present, providing individuals with a means to earn a living and fulfill immediate financial needs. A job may or may not be directly related to one's long-term career goals or personal interests. It often involves fulfilling specific duties and following established protocols within a designated work environment.

3. **Scope and Duration:** One of the key differences between a career and a job lies in their scope and duration. A career spans a significant period, potentially encompassing multiple decades, and involves a progression of roles, experiences, and achievements. It is a lifelong endeavor, allowing individuals to explore different avenues, adapt to changing circumstances, and pursue personal and professional growth. In contrast, a job is typically more short-term and focused on fulfilling immediate employment needs. It may last for weeks, months, or a few years, depending on the specific position or project.

4. **Personal Growth and Development:** A career provides ample opportunities for personal growth and development. It involves acquiring new skills, expanding knowledge, and refining abilities over time. Individuals actively invest in their career development through education, training, networking, and continuous learning. A career is driven by personal aspirations, and individuals strive to achieve their goals, reach higher positions, and make a meaningful impact in their chosen field. In contrast, a job may provide limited opportunities for growth beyond the immediate tasks and responsibilities associated with the position.

5. **Alignment with Interests and Values:** Careers are often built around individuals' interests, passions, and values. They allow individuals to pursue work that aligns with their personal preferences and provides a sense of fulfillment and purpose. In a career, there is a greater emphasis on finding meaning and satisfaction in the work being done. Conversely, a job may or may not align with an individual's interests or values. It may primarily serve as a means of earning income or gaining experience while exploring different fields.

6. **Commitment and Investment:** Building a career requires a significant commitment of time, effort, and dedication. It involves

setting long-term goals, making strategic choices, and actively managing one's professional trajectory. Individuals invest in their career through education, training, mentorship, and building a professional network. A career demands perseverance and a willingness to navigate challenges and setbacks. In contrast, a job typically requires a more immediate commitment to perform specific tasks and fulfill responsibilities as outlined by the employer.

7. **Stability and Advancement:** Careers often provide a higher level of stability and opportunities for advancement compared to jobs. As individuals progress in their careers, they gain expertise, assume leadership roles, and become more marketable. Career advancement may involve promotions, salary increases, and expanded responsibilities. Jobs, on the other hand, may be more susceptible to fluctuations in the job market, organizational changes, or project-based employment.

8. **Long-Term Satisfaction:** While a job can provide temporary satisfaction and meet immediate financial needs, long-term satisfaction is more commonly associated with a fulfilling career. Careers allow individuals to pursue work that aligns with their passions and values, leading to a sense of purpose and fulfillment. They provide

opportunities for personal and professional growth, and the sense of accomplishment derived from progressing in a chosen field can contribute to overall life satisfaction.

Understanding the distinction between a career and a job is crucial for individuals seeking meaningful and fulfilling work experiences. A career represents a long-term journey of personal and professional growth, driven by passion, purpose, and continuous development. A job, on the other hand, is a more immediate employment position focused on meeting immediate needs. While a job can be a stepping stone in building a career, it is the strategic alignment of multiple jobs and experiences that shapes a fulfilling and successful career path. By recognizing the difference between a career and a job, individuals can make informed choices, set realistic expectations, and pursue opportunities that align with their long-term aspirations and personal fulfillment.

Common Mistakes to Avoid When Choosing a Career Path

Choosing a career path is a significant decision that can have a lasting impact on our lives. While it's an exciting endeavor, it's essential to approach it with careful consideration and avoid common pitfalls that can hinder our long-term success and satisfaction. Together, we will explore some common mistakes people make when choosing their career paths and provide insights on how to avoid them. By being aware of these pitfalls, you can make more informed decisions and pave the way for a fulfilling and successful professional journey.

1. **Following External Expectations:** One of the most common mistakes individuals make when choosing a career is succumbing to external expectations. Whether it's pressure from parents, society, or cultural norms, basing your career choice solely on others' expectations can lead to unhappiness and a lack of fulfillment. Instead, focus on understanding your own interests, passions, and values when making career decisions.

2. **Lack of Self-Reflection:** A crucial step in choosing a career path is self-reflection. Many individuals fail to take the time to understand their own strengths, weaknesses, and preferences. Without this self-awareness, it becomes challenging to find a career that aligns with your natural talents and abilities. Take the time to assess your interests, skills, and values to guide your career choices effectively.

3. **Narrow Focus:** Limiting your career options to a narrow field or a single job role can be a limiting factor in finding the right path. It's important to keep an open mind and explore a variety of industries and roles. By expanding your horizons, you increase the chances of finding a career that truly

resonates with you and provides opportunities for growth and development.

4. **Neglecting Research and Information Gathering:** Insufficient research and information gathering can lead to poor career choices. It's essential to thoroughly investigate different career options, including educational requirements, job prospects, industry trends, and work-life balance. Utilize online resources, informational interviews, and networking opportunities to gain valuable insights before making a decision.

5. **Pursuing Only Financial Considerations:** While financial stability is important, solely focusing on monetary gains can lead to dissatisfaction in the long run. It's crucial to strike a balance between financial considerations and personal fulfillment. Consider your passions, interests, and values alongside financial aspects when choosing a career path. This will ensure that you find a career that brings both financial security and personal satisfaction.

6. **Fear of Change and Risk Aversion:** Fear of change and a reluctance to take risks can hinder your ability to explore new career paths and seize opportunities. Growth and success often require stepping outside of your comfort zone and embracing uncertainty. Be

open to change, adaptability, and continuous learning. Embrace calculated risks that align with your goals and aspirations.

7. **Unrealistic Expectations:** Having unrealistic expectations about a chosen career path can lead to disappointment and frustration. It's important to have a realistic understanding of the challenges, demands, and potential setbacks that come with your chosen field. Research and connect with professionals already working in the industry to gain a realistic perspective and set achievable goals.

8. **Ignoring Work-Life Balance:** Neglecting to consider work-life balance can have detrimental effects on your overall well-being and happiness. It's crucial to assess how a particular career path aligns with your desired lifestyle. Consider factors such as work hours, travel requirements, and flexibility. Strive to find a career that allows you to maintain a healthy balance between work and personal life.

9. **Lack of Mentorship and Guidance:** Many individuals overlook the importance of mentorship and guidance when choosing a career path. Mentors can provide valuable insights, guidance, and support based on their own experiences. Seek out mentors in your desired field and learn from their wisdom and

expertise. Their guidance can help you avoid potential pitfalls and make informed decisions.

10. **Failure to Reevaluate and Adapt:** Career paths are not set in stone, and it's essential to reevaluate and adapt as you progress in your professional journey. Over time, your interests, goals, and priorities may change. Failing to regularly reassess your career path can lead to stagnation and a lack of fulfillment. Stay open to new opportunities, be willing to make course corrections, and embrace growth and evolution.

Choosing a career path is a significant decision that requires careful consideration and self-reflection. By avoiding common mistakes such as following external expectations, neglecting research, and pursuing only financial considerations, you can make informed decisions that align with your interests, strengths, and values. Embrace self-reflection, seek mentorship, and stay open to change and growth. Remember that your career path is a dynamic and evolving journey, and by staying proactive and adaptable, you can pave the way for a fulfilling and successful professional life.

The Interplay between Careers and Personality

Our personality traits influence various aspects of our lives, including the choices we make and the paths we embark upon. The connection between careers and personality is a fascinating subject that highlights how our unique characteristics shape our professional journeys. Together, we will explore how careers tie in with personality, examining the influence of traits on career choice, job satisfaction, and overall success.

Our careers are a significant part of our lives, shaping our daily experiences, aspirations, and overall well-being. The choices we make in our professional paths have the power to impact our personal fulfillment, job satisfaction, and success. One crucial factor that influences our career trajectories is our personality. Personality encompasses a unique set of traits, behaviors, and characteristics that define who we are as individuals. It influences the way we perceive and interact with the world around us, including our work environments and relationships with colleagues. Understanding the interplay between our personalities and careers can help us make informed decisions and find fulfillment in our chosen paths.

One popular framework used to understand personality is the Big Five model, which includes five broad dimensions: extraversion, agreeableness, conscientiousness, neuroticism, and openness to experience. Each of these dimensions offers insights into our preferences, tendencies, and strengths, ultimately shaping our career preferences and performance.

Extraversion is characterized by sociability, assertiveness, and a preference for external stimuli. Extraverts often thrive in roles that involve social interaction, such as sales, public relations, or teaching. They tend to excel in environments that provide frequent opportunities for networking, teamwork, and public speaking. On the other hand, introverts, who are more reserved and introspective, may prefer careers that allow for independent work, concentration, and in-depth analysis. They may find fulfillment in professions like writing, research, programming, or graphic design. These careers provide the solitude and autonomy that introverts often seek.

Agreeableness reflects our inclination toward cooperation, empathy, and compassion. Individuals high in agreeableness may excel in careers that involve helping others, such as counseling, social work, or healthcare. They are often valued for their ability to foster positive relationships and navigate conflicts with tact and diplomacy. Conscientiousness is associated with reliability, organization, and a strong work ethic. Individuals high in conscientiousness tend to thrive in careers that demand attention to detail, precision, and adherence to deadlines. They may excel in fields such as project management, accounting, or law, where meticulousness and reliability are highly valued.

Neuroticism, or emotional stability, influences our ability to cope with stress and uncertainty. Individuals with lower levels of neuroticism may be well-suited for high-pressure careers, such as emergency response, crisis management, or entrepreneurship. Their ability to remain calm and composed in challenging situations can contribute to their success in these roles. Openness to experience refers to our curiosity, creativity, and willingness to embrace new ideas and perspectives. Those high in openness may find fulfillment in creative fields like art, design, or innovation. They may also thrive in dynamic and flexible work environments that encourage continuous learning and exploration.

1. **Career Choice:** Personality plays a significant role in career choice. Individuals tend to gravitate towards professions that align with their inherent traits and preferences. For instance, extroverted individuals may be drawn to careers in sales, marketing, or public speaking, as these roles provide ample opportunities for social interaction and communication. Introverted individuals, on the other hand, may be more inclined towards careers that allow for independent work and introspection, such as research, writing, or programming. Our personality traits act as guiding forces, leading us towards professions that resonate with our natural inclinations and strengths.

2. **Job Satisfaction:** The alignment between careers and personality is closely tied to job satisfaction. When our careers allow us to utilize our innate talents and align with our

personality traits, we are more likely to experience higher levels of job satisfaction. For example, individuals who possess a high need for autonomy may find fulfillment in careers that offer flexibility and independence. Similarly, individuals with a strong drive for achievement may thrive in careers that provide challenging goals and opportunities for growth. Job satisfaction arises when our work environment and tasks complement our personality, enabling us to express ourselves authentically and perform at our best.

3. **Performance and Success:** The interplay between careers and personality also impacts our performance and success. When we are engaged in work that aligns with our personality traits, we are more likely to excel and achieve success. For instance, individuals who are detail-oriented and analytical may thrive in careers that require precision and critical thinking, such as accounting or data analysis. Similarly, individuals with strong leadership skills and assertiveness may excel in managerial or entrepreneurial roles. By leveraging our unique personality traits, we can unlock our full potential and achieve professional success in our chosen fields.

4. **Work Environment:** Personality influences not only our career choices but also our preferences for work environments. Some individuals thrive in fast-paced, dynamic settings, while others prefer calm and structured environments. Personality traits such as openness to experience, tolerance for ambiguity, and adaptability shape our preferences for work environments. Understanding our personality allows us to seek out work settings that provide the optimal conditions for our productivity and well-being.

5. **Interpersonal Dynamics:** Personality traits also influence how we interact with others in the workplace. Extroverted individuals, who gain energy from social interactions, may excel in collaborative roles that require frequent teamwork and networking. Introverted individuals, on the other hand, may excel in roles that allow for independent work or require deep focus and analysis. Understanding our personality traits helps us navigate and adapt to different communication styles and work effectively with colleagues, clients, and stakeholders.

The connection between careers and personality is a complex and dynamic interplay that shapes our professional journeys. Our personality traits influence our career choices, job satisfaction, performance, work environment preferences, and interpersonal dynamics. By recognizing and embracing our unique characteristics, we can align our careers with our authentic selves, leading to fulfillment, success, and a sense of purpose in our professional lives. Understanding the interplay between careers and personality allows us to make informed decisions, pursue paths that resonate with our strengths, and create a fulfilling and meaningful career trajectory.

It's important to note that these dimensions represent broad tendencies, and individuals are complex beings with unique combinations of traits. It is rare for someone to fit neatly into a single personality category, as we each possess a blend of traits that shape our individuality. Moreover, the interplay between personality and careers is not limited to the Big Five model. Other personality frameworks, such as the Myers-Briggs Type Indicator (MBTI), also offer insights into career preferences and compatibility.

Furthermore, to the Big Five dimensions, other aspects of personality, such as values, interests, and strengths, also come into play when considering career choices. Personal values, such as a desire for autonomy, a commitment to social justice, or a passion for creativity, can guide individuals toward careers that align with their core beliefs. Interests and strengths, such as a fascination with numbers, a talent for problem-solving, or a love for nature, can lead individuals to pursue careers in fields like finance, engineering, or environmental science. It is essential to consider the interplay between our personalities and careers when making decisions about our professional paths. By understanding our unique traits, preferences, and strengths, we can choose careers that align with who we are at our core, fostering a sense of purpose, engagement, and satisfaction. Self-awareness and introspection, supported by tools like personality assessments and career counseling, can provide valuable insights and guide us toward making informed choices.

The interplay between careers and personality is a complex and dynamic relationship that influences our professional satisfaction and success. By understanding our personality traits, including dimensions like extraversion, agreeableness, conscientiousness, neuroticism, and openness to experience, we can gain valuable insights into our career preferences and strengths. Considering factors such as values, interests, and strengths in conjunction with personality can help us make informed decisions that lead to fulfilling and rewarding career paths. Embracing self-awareness and seeking guidance when needed can empower us to navigate the interplay between careers and personality, ultimately shaping a future that aligns with our true selves.

CHAPTER TWO

Best Career Based on Personality

Our personalities play a significant role in shaping our preferences, behaviors, and interactions with the world around us. When it comes to choosing a career, understanding our personality type is crucial in finding a path that aligns with our natural tendencies and maximizes our potential for success and satisfaction. Together, we will explore the best career options for introverts and extroverts, providing insights and suggestions for each personality type.

Choosing a career path that aligns with our personality is crucial for long-term fulfillment and success. Our personality traits influence how we interact with the world and what work environments suit us best. Introverts and extroverts have distinct preferences and strengths, and understanding these can guide us towards finding the best career fit.

Introverts tend to draw their energy from within and thrive in quieter, more solitary environments. They prefer introspection and focused work. Careers such as writing and editing, research and analysis, IT and programming, graphic design and artistic fields, and counseling and psychology are well-suited for introverts. These paths allow introverts to express their thoughts and creativity, work independently, and make a meaningful impact on others' lives.

On the other hand, extroverts thrive on social interactions and gain energy from being around others. They enjoy collaborative environments and are outgoing and talkative. Careers such as sales and marketing, public relations and event management, teaching and training, human resources and people management, and entertainment and performing arts are ideal for extroverts. These paths enable extroverts to leverage their communication skills, build relationships, inspire others, and showcase their talents.

I. Introverts:

Introverts tend to draw their energy from within and thrive in quieter, more solitary environments. They often prefer introspection, focused work, and one-on-one interactions. Here are some career paths that are well-suited for introverts:

1. **Writing and Editing:** Introverts often possess excellent writing and communication skills. Careers in writing and editing, such as authors, journalists, bloggers, or content creators, allow introverts to express their thoughts and ideas in a solitary setting. These professions provide the necessary solitude and freedom for introverts to work at their own pace and dive deep into their creative process.

2. **Research and Analysis:** Introverts' ability to concentrate and analyze information makes

them well-suited for research-based careers. Fields such as market research, data analysis, scientific research, or academia offer introverts the opportunity to examine intellectual pursuits and work independently. These roles provide a quiet and focused environment that introverts thrive in.

3. **IT and Programming:** The field of information technology (IT) and programming often attracts introverts due to its technical nature and independent work style. Introverts excel in tasks that require deep focus and problem-solving skills, making careers as software developers, database administrators, or cybersecurity experts an excellent fit for their analytical and detail-oriented nature.

4. **Graphic Design and Artistic Careers:** Introverts often possess a keen eye for detail and a strong sense of aesthetics. Careers in graphic design, illustration, photography, or other artistic fields allow introverts to channel their creativity into visual expressions. These professions offer the solitude and creative freedom introverts seek, providing an ideal environment for their imaginative and artistic abilities.

5. **Counseling and Psychology:** Despite introverts' preference for solitude, they often excel in one-on-one interactions, particularly

in a supportive and empathetic capacity. Careers as counselors, therapists, psychologists, or social workers enable introverts to utilize their listening skills and offer guidance to individuals seeking help. These roles provide a quiet and intimate setting where introverts can make a meaningful impact on others' lives.

II. Extroverts:

Extroverts, on the other hand, thrive on social interactions and gain energy from being around others. They are often outgoing, talkative, and enjoy collaborative environments. Here are some career paths that are well-suited for extroverts:

1. **Sales and Marketing:** Extroverts' natural charisma and ability to connect with people make them well-suited for sales and marketing roles. Whether in direct sales, account management, or marketing strategy, extroverts excel in building relationships, networking, and persuading others. These careers provide the social stimulation and fast-paced nature that energize extroverts.

2. **Public Relations and Event Management:** Extroverts thrive in roles that involve public speaking, networking, and organizing events. Careers in public relations, event planning, or hospitality management allow extroverts to leverage their excellent communication skills

and their ability to engage with diverse groups of people. These professions offer ample opportunities for extroverts to showcase their social prowess.

3. **Teaching and Training:** Extroverts' natural enthusiasm and ability to engage with others make them excellent teachers and trainers. Whether in primary education, corporate training, or coaching, extroverts excel in sharing knowledge and guiding others. These careers offer constant interaction, energizing extroverts as they facilitate learning and inspire others.

4. **Human Resources and People Management:** Extroverts' ability to connect with others and understand their needs makes them well-suited for roles in human resources and people management. Whether in recruitment, employee engagement, or leadership development, extroverts thrive in positions that involve understanding and nurturing the potential of individuals. These professions allow extroverts to build strong relationships within organizations.

5. **Entertainment and Performing Arts:** Extroverts often feel at home in the limelight, making careers in entertainment and performing arts a natural fit. Whether in acting, singing, dancing, or hosting, extroverts thrive in careers that allow them to

express themselves and captivate audiences. These professions provide the social interaction and excitement that extroverts crave.

Choosing a career that aligns with your personality is vital for long-term satisfaction and success. Introverts and extroverts have distinct preferences and strengths that can guide them towards careers that complement their natural tendencies. By understanding yourself and considering the characteristics of different professions, you can make informed decisions and find a career path that brings out the best in you. Remember, while personality plays a significant role, individual interests, skills, and values should also be taken into account when making career choices.

Understanding our personality type helps us make informed decisions about our careers. It allows us to capitalize on our strengths, work in environments that energize us, and avoid situations that drain our energy. When we choose a career that aligns with our personality, we are more likely to experience job satisfaction, perform at our best, and achieve long-term success.

However, it's important to note that personality is just one aspect to consider when choosing a career. Other factors such as interests, values, skills, and market demand should also be taken into account. Additionally, individuals can possess a mix of introverted and extroverted traits, making it important to find a balance that suits our unique personalities.

Selecting the best career based on personality requires self-awareness and an understanding of our preferences and strengths. Introverts thrive in quiet, solitary settings and can excel in fields such as writing, research, and counseling. Extroverts thrive in social environments and can thrive in careers like sales, teaching, and entertainment. By aligning our career choices with our personality traits, we increase the likelihood of finding fulfillment, success, and a sense of purpose in our professional lives.

Career Path and Zodiac Signs – Introverts and Extroverts

Zodiac signs have long been associated with various aspects of our lives, including personality traits and compatibility. Many people believe that the alignment of the stars at the time of our birth can influence our character and behavior. In the world of careers, understanding our personality traits and preferences is crucial in finding the right path for ourselves. Together, we will explore the relationship between career paths and zodiac signs, specifically focusing on introverts and extroverts. We will discuss how the characteristics of each sign align with different career choices, helping individuals navigate their professional journey.

Before examine the connection between zodiac signs and career paths, it is important to understand the basic differences between introverts and extroverts. Introverts are typically described as individuals who gain energy from solitude and quiet reflection. They tend to be introspective, preferring deep conversations over small talk and valuing their own inner thoughts and feelings. Extroverts, on the other hand, thrive in social settings and gain energy from being around others. They are outgoing, talkative, and enjoy engaging with people and the external world.

While introversion and extraversion exist on a spectrum, most individuals lean more towards one end or the other. Understanding whether you are more introverted or extroverted can help you identify career paths that align with your natural tendencies and preferences.

Introverted Zodiac Signs and Career Paths:

1. **Taurus (April 20 - May 20):** Taurus individuals are known for their practicality, determination, and strong work ethic. They excel in careers that allow them to focus on their own tasks and work independently. Some suitable career paths for Taurus introverts include accountancy, financial analysis, research, or writing. These roles provide the solitude and space Taurus individuals need to concentrate and excel.

2. **Virgo (August 23 - September 22):** Virgos are detail-oriented, analytical, and have a strong sense of responsibility. They thrive in careers that require precision and meticulousness. Suitable career paths for Virgo introverts include data analysis, quality control, editing, or scientific research. These roles allow Virgos to utilize their sharp analytical skills and attention to detail in a focused and independent manner.

3. **Scorpio (October 23 - November 21):** Scorpios are known for their intensity, deep thinking, and emotional depth. They excel in careers that require them to dive into complex subjects and probe beneath the surface. Suitable career paths for Scorpio introverts include psychology, investigative journalism, research, or forensic science. These roles allow Scorpios to satisfy their curiosity and explore the depths of their chosen field.

4. **Capricorn (December 22 - January 19):** Capricorns are ambitious, disciplined, and thrive in structured environments. They excel in careers that allow them to climb the ladder of success through hard work and perseverance. Suitable career paths for Capricorn introverts include business management, project management, finance, or law. These roles provide Capricorns with

opportunities for growth, leadership, and autonomy.

5. **Pisces (February 19 - March 20):** Pisces individuals are creative, intuitive, and empathetic. They excel in careers that allow them to express their artistic abilities and connect with others on an emotional level. Suitable career paths for Pisces introverts include writing, counseling, music, or social work. These roles provide Pisces individuals with the space to tap into their imagination, compassion, and intuitive abilities.

Extroverted Zodiac Signs and Career Paths:

1. **Aries (March 21 - April 19):** Aries individuals are energetic, assertive, and natural-born leaders. They thrive in careers that allow them to take charge, make quick decisions, and be at the forefront of action. Suitable career paths for Aries extroverts include entrepreneurship, sales, marketing, or sports coaching. These roles provide Aries individuals with the opportunity to showcase their leadership skills, charisma, and competitive spirit.

2. **Gemini (May 21 - June 20):** Geminis are known for their versatility, communication skills, and intellectual curiosity. They excel in careers that require adaptability, social interaction, and continuous learning. Suitable

career paths for Gemini extroverts include journalism, public relations, teaching, or event planning. These roles provide Geminis with opportunities to engage with others, utilize their communication skills, and satisfy their thirst for knowledge.

3. **Leo (July 23 - August 22):** Leos are confident, charismatic, and natural performers. They thrive in careers that allow them to be in the spotlight and showcase their talents. Suitable career paths for Leo extroverts include acting, public speaking, entertainment, or marketing. These roles provide Leos with opportunities to express their creativity, engage with others, and receive recognition for their achievements.

4. **Libra (September 23 - October 22):** Libras are known for their diplomacy, charm, and strong sense of justice. They excel in careers that require interpersonal skills, negotiation abilities, and a sense of balance. Suitable career paths for Libra extroverts include law, human resources, customer relations, or diplomacy. These roles provide Libras with opportunities to work with people, build harmonious relationships, and advocate for fairness and equality.

5. **Sagittarius (November 22 - December 21):** Sagittarius individuals are adventurous, optimistic, and have a thirst for knowledge

and new experiences. They thrive in careers that allow them to explore, travel, and expand their horizons. Suitable career paths for Sagittarius extroverts include travel blogging, international relations, outdoor guiding, or teaching abroad. These roles provide Sagittarius individuals with the opportunity to combine their love for adventure with their outgoing nature.

It's important to note that while these career paths align with certain zodiac signs, individual preferences, skills, and experiences also play a significant role in career choices. The zodiac sign is just one aspect to consider when exploring career options. It is crucial to self-reflect, identify personal strengths, and align them with a career path that brings fulfillment and satisfaction.

Understanding our personality traits, including whether we lean towards introversion or extraversion, can be valuable when it comes to making career choices. By exploring the characteristics associated with each zodiac sign and the corresponding career paths, individuals can gain insights into the types of roles that align with their natural tendencies. However, it's important to remember that these connections are not definitive, and personal interests, skills, and experiences should also be taken into account when choosing a career. Ultimately, the most fulfilling career path is one that resonates with an individual's passions, values, and aspirations, regardless of their zodiac sign.

Cancer Zodiac Signs, Introversion/Extraversion – Career Path

Cancer is the fourth sign of the zodiac and is associated with individuals born between June 21 and July 22. People born under the Cancer sign are known for their emotional depth, intuition, and nurturing nature. When considering career paths for Cancers, it's essential to take into account their introverted or extroverted tendencies, as this can influence the type of work environment in which they thrive. Let's explore some career paths that align with both introverted and extroverted Cancers.

Introverted Cancers:

1. **Counseling/Psychotherapy:** Introverted Cancers have a natural ability to empathize with others and provide emotional support. A career in counseling or psychotherapy allows them to utilize their intuitive and compassionate nature to help individuals navigate through their emotions and challenges.

2. **Writing/Content Creation:** Cancers possess a deep emotional intelligence and excellent communication skills. They often find solace in expressing their thoughts and feelings through writing. Careers in writing, such as journalism, blogging, or content creation, provide introverted Cancers with a

creative outlet to share their perspectives and connect with others.

3. **Research/Analysis:** Introverted Cancers are detail-oriented and analytical. They excel in roles that require careful examination and research. Careers in market research, data analysis, or scientific research allow introverted Cancers to leverage their analytical skills and contribute to making informed decisions.

4. **Graphic Design/Illustration:** Cancers have a strong sense of creativity and imagination. They often find joy in artistic pursuits. Careers in graphic design, illustration, or creative branding provide introverted Cancers with the opportunity to express their artistic flair and bring their ideas to life.

5. **Library Sciences:** Introverted Cancers appreciate quiet and peaceful environments. Careers in library sciences, archiving, or curating allow them to work in serene settings while engaging with knowledge and helping others access valuable resources.

Extroverted Cancers:

1. **Nursing:** Extroverted Cancers have a natural inclination towards caring for others. They thrive in roles that involve human interaction and making a difference in people's lives.

Nursing, with its focus on patient care and providing support, allows extroverted Cancers to use their nurturing qualities to help others.

2. **Teaching/Education:** Extroverted Cancers have a warm and engaging personality, making them excellent teachers. They enjoy sharing knowledge and connecting with students. Careers in teaching, mentoring, or educational administration allow extroverted Cancers to create a positive impact and foster growth in others.

3. **Event Planning/Coordination:** Extroverted Cancers have excellent organizational skills and enjoy bringing people together. Careers in event planning or coordination provide opportunities for extroverted Cancers to utilize their attention to detail and interpersonal skills to create memorable experiences for others.

4. **Public Relations/Marketing:** Extroverted Cancers excel in roles that involve communication and building relationships. Careers in public relations, marketing, or customer relations allow them to leverage their excellent interpersonal skills to represent brands, engage with people, and promote products or services.

5. **Hospitality/Service Industry:** Extroverted Cancers thrive in environments that involve social interaction. Careers in the hospitality industry, such as hotel management, restaurant ownership, or customer service, allow them to use their warm and welcoming nature to provide exceptional experiences to guests.

It's important to remember that these career paths are general suggestions and should be considered alongside individual skills, interests, and aspirations. Additionally, not all Cancers fit neatly into the introverted or extroverted categories, as personality traits can vary among individuals. It's crucial for individuals to reflect on their own preferences, strengths, and values when choosing a career path, regardless of their zodiac sign.

Aries Zodiac Signs, Career Paths, and Introversion/Extraversion

The zodiac sign of Aries, born between March 21 and April 19, is associated with traits such as confidence, ambition, and assertiveness. These characteristics can influence the career paths that Aries individuals may find fulfilling. Additionally, understanding the introversion and extraversion tendencies within the Aries personality can further refine career choices. Aries individuals are often known for their leadership qualities and their ability to take initiative. They possess a natural drive and determination to succeed, which can propel them towards careers that require assertiveness, decision-making skills, and a competitive edge. Aries individuals thrive in environments that allow them to be at the forefront, take charge, and lead others.

For Aries individuals who lean towards introversion, career paths that offer independence, focus, and the opportunity to work autonomously may be appealing. They may find satisfaction in roles that allow them to examine deep research, analysis, or creative work. Careers such as writing, research, graphic design, programming, or entrepreneurship may provide the solitude and flexibility that introverted Aries individual's desire. On the other hand, extraverted Aries individuals thrive in careers that involve interaction, communication, and networking. They excel in roles that allow them to showcase their leadership skills, persuasive abilities, and natural charisma. Careers in sales, marketing, public relations, event management, or entrepreneurship can provide the social stimulation and external validation that extraverted Aries individuals seek.

Aries individuals have a strong entrepreneurial spirit and a desire to be their own boss. They are often not afraid to take risks and explore new opportunities. Starting their own business or pursuing a career in a field where they can exercise their innovative ideas and creativity can be highly rewarding for Aries individuals. Their self-motivation and determination can drive them to succeed in entrepreneurial endeavors. In terms of specific career paths, Aries individuals may excel in professions that require quick decision-making, problem-solving, and a fast-paced environment. They may find success in fields such as management, entrepreneurship, politics, law enforcement, sports, or the military. These careers allow Aries individuals to channel their energy, competitive nature, and drive for achievement into tangible outcomes.

It's important to note that while the zodiac sign of Aries provides general characteristics and tendencies, individuals are complex beings with unique personalities. Not all Aries individuals will fit perfectly into these career suggestions. Factors such as individual interests, skills, values, and educational background should also be taken into consideration when choosing a career path.

Aries individuals can benefit from reflecting on their introversion or extraversion tendencies and how they impact their career preferences. Understanding their own temperament can help them make informed decisions about the work environment, level of social interaction, and independence they desire in their careers. By aligning their personality traits with their chosen career paths, Aries individuals can enhance their professional satisfaction and maximize their potential for success.

Libra Zodiac Signs, Career Paths, and Introversion/Extraversion

Libra, born between September 23 and October 22, is the zodiac sign associated with traits such as diplomacy, balance, and harmony. Individuals born under the sign of Libra often possess strong interpersonal skills, a love for aesthetics, and a desire for fairness. These characteristics influence the career paths that Libra individuals may find fulfilling. Understanding the introversion and extraversion tendencies within the Libra personality can further refine career choices.

Libra individuals thrive in careers that involve working with others and fostering harmonious relationships. They have a natural ability to see different perspectives, mediate conflicts, and find common ground. Careers in law, diplomacy, mediation, counseling, human resources, or social work may align well with their diplomatic nature and desire to promote fairness and justice.

Extraverted Libra individuals are energized by social interactions and enjoy collaborating with others. They have excellent communication skills and can easily build connections with people from various backgrounds. Careers in sales, marketing, public relations, event planning, or customer service may provide the social stimulation and opportunity to build relationships that extraverted Libra individuals seek.

On the other hand, introverted Libra individuals may find satisfaction in careers that allow them to work independently and focus on their creative pursuits. They have a keen eye for aesthetics and often possess artistic talents. Careers in interior design, graphic design, writing, photography, or music composition can provide the solitude and space for introverted Libra individuals to express their creativity and create visually appealing work.

Introverted Libra individuals often possess a deep appreciation for beauty and a desire to create harmony in their surroundings. They may prefer to work behind the scenes, dedicating their time and energy to create aesthetically pleasing environments or products. Fields like architecture, fashion design, landscape design, or curatorial work can provide the platform for introverted Libra individuals to showcase their talents while maintaining a level of privacy and focus.

Libra individuals have a natural ability to bring people together and create a sense of balance and cooperation. They possess strong negotiation and problem-solving skills, making them well-suited for careers that involve resolving conflicts and finding mutually beneficial solutions. Careers in law, mediation, consulting, project management, or leadership positions within organizations can allow Libra individuals to utilize their diplomatic nature and bring about positive change.

It's important to note that while the zodiac sign of Libra provides general characteristics and tendencies, individuals are complex beings with unique personalities. Not all Libra individuals will fit perfectly into these career suggestions. Factors such as individual interests, skills, values, and educational background should also be taken into consideration when choosing a career path.

Libra individuals can benefit from reflecting on their introversion or extraversion tendencies and how they impact their career preferences. Understanding their own temperament can help them make informed decisions about the level of social interaction, creative outlets, and opportunities for promoting harmony they desire in their careers. By aligning their personality traits with their chosen career paths, Libra individuals can enhance their professional satisfaction and maximize their potential for success.

Gemini Zodiac Signs, Career Paths, and Introversion/Extraversion

Gemini, born between May 21 and June 20, is the zodiac sign associated with traits such as versatility, curiosity, and adaptability. Individuals born under the sign of Gemini often possess excellent communication skills, a quick wit, and a thirst for knowledge. These characteristics influence the career paths that Gemini individuals may find fulfilling. Understanding the introversion and extraversion tendencies within the Gemini personality can further refine career choices. Gemini individuals are known for their exceptional communication skills and love for social interaction. They thrive in careers that involve frequent interaction with others, whether it's through verbal or written communication. Roles in journalism, public relations, marketing, sales, or customer service can provide the social stimulation and variety that extraverted Gemini individuals seek.

Extraverted Gemini individuals often excel in roles that require adaptability, flexibility, and the ability to multitask. They are quick thinkers who can handle multiple projects simultaneously and navigate rapidly changing situations. Careers in event planning, project management, advertising, or entertainment may suit their dynamic nature and need for constant mental stimulation. On the other hand, introverted Gemini individuals may find satisfaction in careers that allow them to focus on deep research, analysis, or creative work. They have a keen intellect and a natural curiosity that drives them to explore and learn. Careers such as writing, editing, research analysis, programming, or graphic design can provide the solitude and independence that introverted Gemini individuals' desire.

Introverted Gemini individuals often possess excellent analytical skills and attention to detail. They thrive in environments where they can examine complex problems, work independently, and bring their creative ideas to life. Fields like technology, data analysis, research, or academia may align well with their introverted tendencies and desire for intellectual stimulation. Gemini individuals have a natural ability to adapt to new situations and embrace change. They possess excellent communication skills, which allow them to convey ideas effectively and connect with others on various levels. This adaptability makes them well-suited for careers that involve travel, international relations, teaching, consulting, or diplomacy.

Gemini individuals are often drawn to careers that allow them to express their creativity and intellect. They enjoy engaging in intellectually stimulating work that challenges their minds and allows them to constantly learn and grow. Careers in writing, journalism, acting, teaching, or research can provide the platform for Gemini individuals to express their ideas and showcase their natural talents. It's important to note that while the zodiac sign of Gemini provides general characteristics and tendencies, individuals are complex beings with unique personalities. Not all Gemini individuals will fit perfectly into these career suggestions. Factors such as individual interests, skills, values, and educational background should also be taken into consideration when choosing a career path.

Ultimately, Gemini individuals can benefit from reflecting on their introversion or extraversion tendencies and how they impact their career preferences. Understanding their own temperament can help them make informed decisions about the level of social interaction, intellectual stimulation, and variety they desire in their careers. By aligning their personality traits with their chosen career paths, Gemini individuals can enhance their professional satisfaction and maximize their potential for success.

Leo Zodiac Signs, Career Paths, and Introversion/Extraversion

Leo, born between July 23 and August 22, is the zodiac sign associated with traits such as confidence, ambition, and charisma. Individuals born under the sign of Leo often possess strong leadership qualities, a desire for recognition, and a creative flair. These characteristics influence the career paths that Leo individuals may find fulfilling. Understanding the introversion and extraversion tendencies within the Leo personality can further refine career choices.

Leo individuals thrive in careers that allow them to shine and be in the spotlight. They possess natural leadership abilities and are often driven to take charge and guide others. They excel in roles that involve managing teams, leading projects, or spearheading initiatives. Careers in management, entrepreneurship, politics, entertainment, or the performing arts can provide the platform for Leo individuals to express their talents and fulfill their need for recognition. Extraverted Leo individuals are energized by social interactions and enjoy being the center of attention. They have excellent communication skills and can captivate others with their persuasive abilities and natural charisma. Careers in sales, marketing, public relations, event management, or the media may align well with their extraverted nature and desire for external validation.

On the other hand, introverted Leo individuals may find satisfaction in careers that allow them to focus on their creative pursuits or work independently. They have a strong sense of self-expression and enjoy exploring their artistic talents. Careers in writing, graphic design, photography, interior design, or music production can provide the solitude and space for introverted Leo individuals to channel their creativity. Introverted Leo individuals often possess a deep passion for their craft and a desire to create meaningful work. They may prefer to work behind the scenes, dedicating their time and energy to perfecting their skills and producing exceptional results. Fields like filmmaking, animation, editing, or writing can provide the platform for introverted Leo individuals to showcase their talents while maintaining a level of privacy and focus.

Leo individuals have a natural ability to inspire and motivate others. They possess a strong sense of purpose and often seek careers that allow them to make a positive impact and lead by example. Careers in coaching, mentoring, motivational speaking, or education can provide the platform for Leo individuals to inspire and uplift others while utilizing their leadership abilities. It's important to note that while the zodiac sign of Leo provides general characteristics and tendencies, individuals are complex beings with unique personalities. Not all Leo individuals will fit perfectly into these career suggestions. Factors such as individual interests, skills, values, and educational background should also be taken into consideration when choosing a career path.

Leo individuals can benefit from reflecting on their introversion or extraversion tendencies and how they impact their career preferences. Understanding their own temperament can help them make informed decisions about the level of social interaction, leadership opportunities, and creative outlets they desire in their careers. By aligning their personality traits with their chosen career paths, Leo individuals can enhance their professional satisfaction and maximize their potential for success.

Sagittarius Zodiac Signs, Career Paths, and Introversion/Extraversion

Sagittarius, born between November 22 and December 21, is the zodiac sign associated with traits such as adventure, optimism, and intellectual curiosity. Individuals born under the sign of Sagittarius often possess a love for exploration, a desire for personal freedom, and a thirst for knowledge. These characteristics influence the career paths that Sagittarius individuals may find fulfilling. Understanding the introversion and extraversion tendencies within the Sagittarius personality can further refine career choices.

Sagittarius individuals thrive in careers that allow them to explore new territories and expand their horizons. They possess a sense of adventure and a natural curiosity about the world. Careers in travel, journalism, photography, international relations, or outdoor activities may align well with their need for exploration and their desire to experience new cultures and environments.

Extraverted Sagittarius individuals are energized by social interactions and enjoy being in the company of others. They have excellent communication skills and can easily connect with people from different backgrounds. Careers in public speaking, teaching, sales, marketing, or event management may provide the social stimulation and opportunities for networking that extraverted Sagittarius individuals seek.

On the other hand, introverted Sagittarius individuals may find satisfaction in careers that allow them to examine deep intellectual pursuits and work independently. They have a strong desire for personal freedom and may enjoy careers that allow them to set their own schedules and explore their interests without strict structures. Fields like writing, research, philosophy, programming, or entrepreneurship can provide the solitude and autonomy that introverted Sagittarius individuals desire.

Introverted Sagittarius individuals often possess a deep love for learning and a desire to seek truth and meaning. They may prefer to work behind the scenes, dedicating their time and energy to studying and acquiring knowledge. Careers in academia, research, writing, or consulting can provide the platform for introverted Sagittarius individuals to examine their intellectual pursuits and contribute to the expansion of knowledge.

Sagittarius individuals have a natural ability to inspire others and often possess a strong sense of purpose. They enjoy careers that allow them to make a positive impact and encourage personal growth in themselves and others. Careers in coaching, mentoring, motivational speaking, education, or humanitarian work may align well with their desire to uplift and empower others.

It's important to note that while the zodiac sign of Sagittarius provides general characteristics and tendencies, individuals are complex beings with unique personalities. Not all Sagittarius individuals will fit perfectly into these career suggestions. Factors such as individual interests, skills, values, and educational background should also be taken into consideration when choosing a career path.

Sagittarius individuals can benefit from reflecting on their introversion or extraversion tendencies and how they impact their career preferences. Understanding their own temperament can help them make informed decisions about the level of social interaction, freedom, and intellectual stimulation they desire in their careers. By aligning their personality traits with their chosen career paths, Sagittarius individuals can enhance their professional satisfaction and maximize their potential for success.

Best-Paying Careers for Introverts:

Introverts often thrive in careers that allow for independent work, require deep focus, and minimize extensive social interactions. Introverts, who typically thrive in quiet and solitary environments, often find themselves seeking careers that allow them to work independently and engage in deep, focused work. While introverts may prefer less social interaction, it doesn't mean they can't excel in high-paying careers. In fact, there are numerous lucrative career paths that cater to the strengths and preferences of introverted individuals. While it is important to note that individual preferences and aptitudes vary, here are some of the best paying careers that tend to align well with the strengths and inclinations of introverts:

1. **Software Developer:** Software development offers excellent career prospects and high earning potential. Introverts can leverage their analytical and problem-solving skills to design, develop, and test software applications. This career allows for independent work and deep focus, with limited need for extensive social interactions.

2. **Data Scientist:** Data science has emerged as a lucrative field in recent years. Data scientists analyze and interpret complex data

to uncover patterns and insights, helping organizations make informed decisions. This career involves working with data sets, programming, and statistical analysis, making it an ideal fit for introverts who enjoy working independently and examine data.

3. **Financial Analyst:** Financial analysts analyze investment opportunities, assess financial performance, and provide insights and recommendations to clients or organizations. This career requires strong analytical skills, attention to detail, and the ability to work independently. Introverts can excel in this field, utilizing their analytical thinking and research abilities.

4. **Accountant:** Accounting is a stable and well-paying profession. Accountants handle financial records, perform audits, and provide financial advice to individuals and businesses. This career requires precision, analytical thinking, and the ability to work independently, making it suitable for introverts who enjoy working with numbers and data.

5. **Graphic Designer:** Graphic design offers a creative outlet for introverts. Graphic designers create visual concepts and design materials for various purposes, including branding, marketing, and web design. This career allows for independent work and

provides opportunities to express creativity through visual communication.

6. **Technical Writer:** Technical writing involves creating documentation, user guides, and instructional materials for complex technical concepts. Introverts with strong writing and communication skills can excel in this field, as it requires attention to detail, research, and the ability to explain technical information clearly.

7. **Research Scientist:** Research scientists work in various fields, such as biology, chemistry, or physics, conducting experiments, analyzing data, and publishing findings. This career allows introverts to examine deep into their areas of interest, working independently in research laboratories or academic institutions.

8. **Archivist:** Archivists manage and preserve historical documents and records. They organize and catalog materials, curate collections, and provide access to information. This career involves working independently, organizing information, and ensuring its preservation for future generations.

9. **Statistician:** Statisticians collect and analyze data to solve problems and make informed decisions in various industries. This field

requires strong analytical skills, mathematical proficiency, and the ability to work independently. Introverts can thrive in this career, working behind the scenes to uncover meaningful insights from data.

10. **Actuary:** Actuaries assess and manage financial risks for insurance companies and other organizations. They use mathematical models and statistical analysis to determine the likelihood of future events. This career requires strong analytical and problem-solving skills, making it suitable for introverts who enjoy working with numbers and complex calculations.

It's important to note that while these careers tend to align well with introverted tendencies, individual preferences and aptitudes vary. It is crucial for introverts to consider their personal interests, strengths, and work preferences when choosing a career path. It's important to note that while these careers are well-suited for introverts, individual interests, skills, and educational background should also be taken into consideration when choosing a career path. The key is to find a balance between personal preferences and financial prospects to ensure long-term career satisfaction. By leveraging their unique strengths, introverts can thrive in high-paying careers while enjoying the solitude and deep engagement they desire.

Best-Paying Careers for Extroverts

Extroverts thrive in social environments, drawing energy from interactions with others. They excel in roles that involve communication, collaboration, and engaging with people. Together, we will explore some of the best-paying careers that align well with the strengths and preferences of extroverts. While individual interests and aptitudes may vary, these careers offer excellent earning potential and ample opportunities for extroverts to leverage their social energy and interpersonal skills. Extroverts thrive on social interactions, love being the center of attention, and find energy in the company of others. They excel in careers that allow them to express their outgoing and sociable nature. Fortunately, there are numerous high-paying career paths that cater to the strengths and preferences of extroverted individuals.

1. **Sales Manager:** Sales management is a high-paying career that suits the outgoing and persuasive nature of extroverts. Sales managers oversee sales teams, set targets, develop strategies, and build relationships with clients. The ability to connect with people, negotiate, and influence decisions are critical in this role, making it a great fit for extroverts.

2. **Public Relations Manager:** Public relations managers are responsible for maintaining a positive public image for organizations or individuals. They handle media relations,

plan and execute publicity campaigns, and communicate key messages to target audiences. This career requires strong communication skills, networking abilities, and the capacity to thrive in social settings, making it a natural fit for extroverts.

3. **Marketing Manager:** Marketing managers create and implement strategies to promote products or services. They conduct market research, develop marketing campaigns, and manage teams. Extroverts can leverage their interpersonal skills to build relationships with clients, collaborate with cross-functional teams, and effectively communicate brand messages, contributing to the success of marketing initiatives.

4. **Event Planner:** Event planners coordinate and execute various types of events, such as conferences, weddings, and corporate functions. They manage logistics, negotiate with vendors, and ensure the smooth operation of events. This career allows extroverts to showcase their organizational skills, creativity, and ability to engage with clients and attendees, creating memorable experiences.

5. **Human Resources Manager:** Human resources managers oversee the recruitment, training, and development of employees within organizations. They foster a positive

work environment, handle employee relations, and ensure compliance with labor laws and regulations. Strong interpersonal skills, including active listening, conflict resolution, and relationship building, are crucial in this role, making it well-suited for extroverts.

6. **Real Estate Agent:** Real estate agents help individuals buy, sell, or rent properties. They work closely with clients, understand their needs, and guide them through the entire real estate process. Extroverts can leverage their communication skills, charisma, and ability to connect with people to establish trust and close deals successfully, contributing to their financial success.

7. **Advertising Manager:** Advertising managers oversee the development and execution of advertising campaigns. They collaborate with creative teams, analyze market trends, and work with clients to achieve their marketing objectives. This career requires excellent communication skills, creativity, and the ability to work in a fast-paced, dynamic environment—ideal for extroverts who thrive on interaction and collaboration.

8. **Executive Recruiter:** Executive recruiters assist organizations in identifying and hiring top-level executives. They establish

relationships with clients, conduct candidate searches, and facilitate the hiring process. This career involves networking, conducting interviews, and assessing candidates' qualifications and fit for leadership roles. Extroverts can excel in this field by utilizing their networking skills, persuasive abilities, and talent for building professional relationships.

9. **Financial Advisor:** Financial advisors provide guidance on investment decisions, retirement planning, and wealth management to individuals or businesses. They build relationships with clients, understand their financial goals, and offer tailored advice. Extroverts can leverage their communication skills and ability to establish trust to excel in this career, as they engage with clients and navigate complex financial matters.

10. **Entrepreneur:** Entrepreneurship offers extroverts the opportunity to build their own business ventures. The dynamic nature of entrepreneurship allows them to engage with clients, build a network,

Maximizing Potential in College - Introverts

Selecting the right degree program is a crucial decision for introverted individuals in their pursuit of higher education. While personal interests and career goals play a significant role in this decision-making process, introverts often excel in fields that align with their strengths and preferences. Together, we will explore various degree options that are well-suited for introverts, taking into consideration their inclination towards introspection, analytical thinking, and independent work.

It's important to note that while these careers are well-suited for extroverts, individual interests, skills, and educational background should also be taken into consideration when choosing a career path. The key is to find a balance between personal preferences and financial prospects to ensure long-term career satisfaction. By unleashing their social energy and leveraging their strengths, extroverts can thrive in high-paying careers while enjoying the social interactions and dynamic environments they desire.

1. **Psychology:** Psychology is a popular degree choice for introverts due to its emphasis on understanding human behavior and the mind. Introverts' natural inclination towards introspection and empathy can be leveraged in this field, allowing them to excel in areas such as counseling, research, and therapy. The study of psychology provides opportunities for independent research, deep analysis, and a deeper understanding of the complexities of the human mind.

2. **Computer Science:** Computer science offers introverts a perfect balance between analytical thinking and independent work.

Introverted individuals often possess strong problem-solving skills and attention to detail, which are essential in programming and software development. This field provides ample opportunities for introverts to work on complex coding projects, engage in logical reasoning, and contribute to technological advancements.

3. **English Literature:** English literature is an ideal choice for introverts who possess a love for language, literature, and deep analysis. The study of literature allows introverts to immerse themselves in the written word, explore diverse perspectives, and critically analyze complex texts. The solitude and introspection associated with reading and writing align well with introverted tendencies, making this field a natural fit.

4. **Mathematics:** Mathematics is a field that emphasizes logical thinking, problem-solving, and independent work. Introverts often possess strong analytical skills and an affinity for structured, abstract thinking, making mathematics a suitable degree option. The study of mathematics allows introverts to engage in challenging problem sets, explore complex mathematical concepts, and contribute to the development of new mathematical theories.

5. **Environmental Science:** Introverts who have a passion for the environment and a desire to make a positive impact can consider pursuing a degree in environmental science. This field allows individuals to study and analyze the natural world, explore environmental issues, and contribute to sustainable practices. The independent research, data analysis, and fieldwork involved in environmental science provide introverts with opportunities to work autonomously while addressing pressing global challenges.

6. **Graphic Design:** Graphic design combines creativity and technical skills, making it an appealing option for introverts with artistic abilities. Introverted individuals often excel in visually expressing their ideas and concepts, and graphic design provides a platform to do so. This field allows introverts to work independently on design projects, express their creativity through visual communication, and contribute to various industries, including advertising, marketing, and web design.

7. **History:** History appeals to introverts who enjoy examine the past, analyzing historical events, and interpreting their impact on society. The study of history allows introverts to engage in extensive research, critical thinking, and detailed analysis of primary and

secondary sources. This degree offers opportunities for introspection, independent writing, and the exploration of historical narratives.

8. **Library Science:** Library science is a field that aligns well with introverted tendencies, as it involves working in quiet, contemplative environments surrounded by books and information. Introverts often possess strong research skills, attention to detail, and a passion for organizing and categorizing knowledge. Pursuing a degree in library science opens doors to careers as librarians, archivists, or information specialists, allowing introverts to contribute to the preservation and dissemination of information.

9. **Physics:** Physics appeals to introverts with a fascination for understanding the fundamental laws and principles that govern the universe. This field involves extensive research, data analysis, and theoretical exploration. Introverts can excel in physics due to their natural inclination towards introspection, independent study, and the ability to engage in complex problem-solving.

10. **Sociology:** Sociology is a discipline that examines human society, social structures, and the interactions between individuals and

groups. Introverts' skills in observation, critical thinking, and empathy make them well-suited for the study of social dynamics. This field offers opportunities for independent research, qualitative analysis, and a deeper understanding of social issues.

When choosing a degree program, introverts should consider their personal interests, strengths, and preferences. The degrees mentioned above provide a starting point for introverts to explore fields that align with their natural tendencies towards introspection, independent work, and analytical thinking. It is crucial for introverts to find a balance between their personal inclinations and the requirements of their chosen field, ensuring a fulfilling and successful academic journey. By pursuing a degree that resonates with their personality, introverts can maximize their potential and make significant contributions to their chosen fields.

Maximizing Potential: Extroverts in Colleges

Choosing the right degree program is a significant decision for extroverted individuals pursuing higher education. Extroverts thrive in social interactions, collaborative environments, and roles that allow them to utilize their communication and interpersonal skills. Together, we will explore a range of degree options that align well with the strengths and preferences of extroverts, enabling them to maximize their potential and find fulfillment in their academic and professional pursuits.

1. **Communication Studies:** Communication studies offer a comprehensive understanding of interpersonal, organizational, and mass communication. Extroverts excel in this field due to their natural ability to engage with others, communicate effectively, and build relationships. By pursuing a degree in communication studies, extroverts can develop skills in public speaking, persuasion, and media literacy, opening doors to careers in public relations, journalism, event management, and marketing.

2. **Business Administration:** Business administration degrees provide a broad foundation in various business disciplines, including management, marketing, finance, and entrepreneurship. Extroverts can leverage their interpersonal skills, leadership abilities, and networking prowess in this field. They thrive in collaborative environments, making valuable contributions to team projects and building networks that can lead to career opportunities in management, sales, consulting, and entrepreneurship.

3. **Hospitality and Tourism Management:** Extroverts with a passion for travel, customer service, and creating memorable experiences

can pursue a degree in hospitality and tourism management. This field emphasizes interpersonal skills, cultural understanding, and event planning. Extroverts can thrive in roles such as hotel management, event coordination, tourism marketing, and hospitality consulting, where they can engage with diverse individuals and provide exceptional service.

4. **Education:** Education degrees are ideal for extroverts who enjoy working with people, particularly in a teaching or mentoring capacity. They can pursue degrees in early childhood education, elementary education, secondary education, or specialized fields such as special education or physical education. Extroverts can bring energy, enthusiasm, and effective communication skills to the classroom, making a positive impact on students' lives.

5. **Social Work:** Social work degrees focus on addressing social issues, advocating for marginalized populations, and providing support to individuals and communities. Extroverts can channel their empathy, compassion, and strong communication skills into careers in social work. This field offers opportunities to engage with diverse populations, collaborate with multidisciplinary teams, and make a meaningful difference in people's lives.

6. **Theater Arts:** Theater arts degrees cater to extroverts who thrive in creative and performance-based environments. Extroverts often possess a natural flair for dramatic expression, public speaking, and storytelling. Through theater arts programs, they can develop their acting, directing, or production skills, pursuing careers in theater, film, television, or even corporate training and public speaking.

7. **Public Administration:** Public administration degrees prepare individuals for careers in government, nonprofit organizations, and public service. Extroverts can utilize their leadership abilities, networking skills, and passion for making a positive impact on society. This field offers opportunities to engage with diverse communities, manage projects, and address societal challenges through policy development, program management, and community outreach.

8. **Event Management:** Event management programs equip students with the skills to plan, organize, and execute various types of events, such as conferences, weddings, concerts, and corporate functions. Extroverts' natural inclination towards socializing, networking, and managing relationships makes them well-suited for this field. They

can thrive in roles that involve coordinating logistics, working with vendors, and ensuring a seamless event experience.

9. **Public Relations:** Public relations degrees focus on managing communication and building relationships between organizations and their target audiences. Extroverts excel in this field due to their strong interpersonal skills, networking abilities, and persuasive communication styles. They can pursue careers as public relations specialists, media relations managers, or communications consultants, helping organizations navigate public perception and maintain positive brand image.

10. **Sports Management:** Sports management degrees combine business principles with a focus on sports-related industries. Extroverts who have a passion for sports, leadership, and event organization can find fulfilling careers in sports management. They can engage in sports marketing, sports event planning, athlete management, or sports facility management, utilizing their social skills and enthusiasm to contribute to the sports industry.

Extroverts possess natural strengths in communication, collaboration, and building relationships, making them well-suited for a variety of degree programs. The options mentioned above provide extroverts with opportunities to maximize their potential and pursue careers that align with their social energy and interpersonal skills. By selecting degrees that harness their strengths, extroverts can find fulfillment, excel in their chosen fields, and make significant contributions to their professions.

Unleashing the Social Energizers: Extroverts

Extroverts are individuals who thrive in social settings, drawing energy from interactions with others. They possess distinctive characteristics and behaviors that distinguish them from introverts. Together, we will explore the various aspects of extraversion, including its definition, personality traits, strengths, challenges, and the ways in which extroverts navigate the world. By gaining a deeper understanding of extroverts, we can appreciate their unique qualities and appreciate the value they bring to personal and professional relationships.

Definition of Extraversion: Extraversion is one of the five major personality traits identified in the Big Five model of personality. It refers to the tendency to seek external stimulation, gain energy from social interactions, and exhibit assertiveness, enthusiasm, and sociability. Extroverts are energized by being around others, enjoy engaging in conversations, and are comfortable in group settings. They tend to be outgoing, talkative, and expressive in their interactions.

Personality Traits of Extroverts:

1. **Sociability:** Extroverts are naturally inclined to seek social connections and enjoy being in the company of others. They thrive in environments that offer opportunities for socializing, networking, and collaborating with different individuals.

2. **Assertiveness:** Extroverts often exhibit assertiveness and confidence in expressing their thoughts and opinions. They are comfortable taking the lead in social situations, initiating conversations, and asserting themselves in group settings.

3. **Energy Gain from Social Interactions:** Unlike introverts who may feel drained by excessive social interactions, extroverts gain energy from being around people. They are rejuvenated and recharged by social stimuli, making them more likely to seek out social engagements.

4. **Outgoing Nature:** Extroverts tend to have a natural inclination to engage in social activities and express themselves openly. They enjoy meeting new people, attending social events, and are often seen as the life of the party.

5. **Talkativeness:** Extroverts are generally talkative and enjoy expressing their thoughts

and ideas verbally. They have a propensity for engaging in conversations, sharing stories, and actively participating in discussions.

Strengths of Extroverts:

1. **Excellent Communication Skills:** Extroverts possess strong verbal communication skills and are adept at expressing themselves effectively. They often excel in roles that require public speaking, presenting, and persuading others.

2. **Networking Abilities:** Extroverts are skilled at building and maintaining relationships. They have a natural ease in networking situations and can connect with people from diverse backgrounds, making them valuable assets in professional and social settings.

3. **Collaboration and Teamwork:** With their sociable nature, extroverts thrive in collaborative environments. They excel at working in teams, fostering cooperation, and leveraging the strengths of different team members to achieve shared goals.

4. **Positive and Energetic Presence:** Extroverts have a contagious energy and enthusiasm that can uplift those around them. Their positive outlook and ability to create a lively atmosphere can contribute to fostering

a productive and enjoyable work or social environment.

Challenges Faced by Extroverts:

1. **Overstimulation:** Due to their preference for social interactions, extroverts may sometimes find themselves overwhelmed by excessive external stimuli. They may need to find a balance between engaging with others and taking time for solitude and introspection.

2. **Need for Validation:** Extroverts may have a higher need for external validation and recognition. They may seek approval from others or feel a sense of self-worth through social affirmation, which can sometimes lead to dependence on external opinions.

3. **Difficulty with Solitude:** Unlike introverts who recharge by spending time alone, extroverts may find it challenging to be in solitude for extended periods. They may need to learn to embrace moments of quiet reflection and develop strategies to find inner fulfillment.

Navigating the World as an Extrovert:

1. **Recognizing Personal Boundaries:** It is important for extroverts to establish personal boundaries to ensure they do not become overextended. They should be mindful of

balancing social interactions with self-care and creating time for rest and rejuvenation.

2. **Engaging in Meaningful Relationships:** Extroverts thrive on meaningful connections. They should focus on building authentic relationships and nurturing connections with individuals who appreciate and reciprocate their social energy.

3. **Seeking Varied Social Environments:** Extroverts can benefit from seeking diverse social environments that provide opportunities for growth, learning, and exposure to new perspectives. This can broaden their understanding of the world and enhance their interpersonal skills.

4. **Embracing Self-Reflection:** While extroverts are energized by external stimuli, they should also allocate time for self-reflection. Engaging in introspection can help them gain insights into their thoughts, emotions, and personal growth, leading to a more holistic understanding of themselves.

Extroverts are individuals who thrive in social interactions, drawing energy from the external world. Their sociable nature, excellent communication skills, and ability to connect with others make them valuable assets in personal and professional relationships. However, extroverts also face unique challenges, such as overstimulation and a need for external validation. By understanding the traits, strengths, and challenges of extroverts, we can appreciate their contributions to society and create environments that allow them to flourish. Ultimately, embracing and celebrating the diversity of personality types, including extraversion, enriches our collective human experience.

The Power of Solitude: Introverts

Introverts are individuals who thrive in quieter, more introspective environments, where they find solace in solitude and gain energy from internal reflection. They possess unique characteristics and behaviors that set them apart from extroverts. Together, we will examine the world of introverts, exploring their definition, personality traits, strengths, challenges, and the ways in which introverts navigate the world. By gaining a deeper understanding of introversion, we can appreciate the valuable contributions introverts make and create environments that support their needs and potential.

Introversion is one of the major personality traits identified in the Big Five model of personality. It refers to the tendency to focus inwardly, drawing energy from solitary activities and internal reflection. Introverts prefer quieter, less stimulating environments and may find social interactions draining, requiring time alone to recharge.

Personality Traits of Introverts:

1. **Need for Solitude:** Introverts thrive in solitude, finding it essential for recharging and regaining energy. They prefer quieter environments that allow for introspection, reflection, and individual pursuits.

2. **Reserved Nature:** Introverts tend to be more reserved and reserved in their demeanor. They often take time to process information internally before expressing their thoughts or opinions.

3. **Selective Socializing:** While introverts may not seek out extensive social interactions, they still value meaningful connections. They prefer deeper one-on-one or small group interactions over large gatherings, where they can engage in more substantial conversations.

4. **Thoughtful Listening:** Introverts excel in active listening, preferring to absorb information and reflect before responding. They often provide thoughtful insights and contribute to conversations with depth and introspection.

5. **Independent Work Style:** Introverts are comfortable working independently and can focus deeply on tasks. They are self-

motivated, highly productive in solitary settings, and often exhibit strong attention to detail.

Strengths of Introverts:

1. **Deep Thinking and Creativity:** Introverts have a natural inclination towards deep thinking and introspection. They often possess rich inner worlds, which fosters creativity, innovation, and the ability to generate unique ideas.

2. **Strong Observational Skills:** Introverts excel at observing their surroundings and picking up on subtle cues. This attentiveness allows them to notice details that others may overlook, enhancing their problem-solving abilities and attention to nuance.

3. **Reflective Decision Making:** Introverts tend to take their time to make decisions, weighing various perspectives and considering all angles. Their reflective approach often leads to well-thought-out decisions based on careful analysis.

4. **Exceptional Focus and Concentration:** Introverts thrive in quiet, uninterrupted environments, enabling them to maintain high levels of focus and concentration. This attribute allows them to examine deeply into

complex tasks and produce high-quality work.

Challenges Faced by Introverts:

1. **Social Energy Depletion:** Introverts may experience social energy depletion, particularly in highly stimulating or prolonged social situations. They require ample time alone to recharge and regain their energy levels.

2. **Misunderstandings and Misconceptions:** Due to their quieter nature, introverts may be misunderstood as aloof, shy, or uninterested. It is important for others to recognize and respect their need for solitude and understand that introversion is not a flaw or weakness.

3. **Public Speaking and Networking:** Public speaking and networking events can be challenging for introverts, as they may find it overwhelming to engage in large group conversations or speak in front of an audience. However, with practice and preparation, introverts can develop effective public speaking and networking skills.

4. **Advocating for Personal Boundaries:** Introverts often need to assert their need for solitude and communicate their boundaries to ensure they have the time and space they require. This may involve setting aside

designated alone time or politely declining excessive social engagements.

Navigating the World as an Introvert:

1. **Self-Awareness and Self-Acceptance:** Introverts should embrace and accept their introversion as a natural part of their identity. By understanding their needs and preferences, introverts can advocate for themselves and create a lifestyle that supports their well-being.

2. **Nurturing Meaningful Connections:** While introverts may prefer smaller social circles, they can still cultivate deep and meaningful relationships. They should focus on developing connections with individuals who appreciate their introspective nature and provide them with the intellectual and emotional stimulation they seek.

3. **Leveraging Introvert Strengths:** Introverts should identify and leverage their strengths, such as their ability to focus deeply, think critically, and engage in reflective practices. By finding careers and pursuits that align with these strengths, introverts can thrive and make significant contributions.

4. **Finding Balance:** Introverts benefit from finding a balance between solitary pursuits and social interactions. They should allocate

time for self-reflection and solitude while also engaging in social activities that align with their interests and provide meaningful connections.

Introverts possess unique qualities and strengths that contribute to their personal and professional lives. Their preference for solitude, introspection, and depth of thinking brings a valuable perspective to the world. By understanding the nature of introversion, appreciating their strengths, and creating environments that support their needs, we can foster an inclusive society that values and benefits from the contributions of introverts.

CHAPTER THREE

What is DNA?

DNA, short for deoxyribonucleic acid, is a molecule that carries the genetic instructions for the development, functioning, and reproduction of all living organisms. It is a long, double-stranded helical structure located within the cells of living organisms, including plants, animals, and even some viruses. DNA is composed of nucleotides, which are the building blocks of the molecule. Each nucleotide consists of three components: a sugar molecule called deoxyribose, a phosphate group, and a nitrogenous base. There are four types of nitrogenous bases in DNA: adenine (A), thymine (T), cytosine (C), and guanine (G). The specific sequence of these bases along the DNA strand forms the genetic code.

The two DNA strands in a double helix are held together by hydrogen bonds between complementary base pairs. Adenine pairs with thymine (A-T), and cytosine pairs with guanine (C-G). This complementary base pairing is crucial for DNA replication and the transmission of genetic information from one generation to the next. DNA carries genetic information in the form of genes, which are specific segments of DNA that encode instructions for the production of proteins. Proteins are essential molecules that perform various functions in cells, such as catalyzing chemical reactions, providing structure, and regulating gene expression.

The structure and sequence of DNA are fundamental to inheritance and the diversity of life. DNA is replicated during cell division, ensuring that each new cell receives an identical copy of the genetic information. It also undergoes genetic recombination and mutation, contributing to genetic variation and the evolution of species over time. Advancements in DNA research and technology have revolutionized fields such as genetics, genomics, and biotechnology. DNA sequencing techniques allow scientists to determine the precise order of nucleotides in a DNA molecule, enabling the study of genetic diseases, the identification of genetic traits, and the analysis of evolutionary relationships.

DNA is a molecule that stores and transmits genetic information in living organisms. Its structure, composed of nucleotides and base pairs, determines the genetic code that guides the development and functioning of organisms. Understanding DNA is vital for unraveling the mysteries of life, from the basic mechanisms of inheritance to the complexities of genetic diseases and the diversity of species on our planet.

Genetic Connection and Professional Success

The concept of a career path and the intricate workings of DNA may seem unrelated at first glance. However, upon closer examination, it becomes apparent that there are intriguing connections between the two. Our DNA holds the blueprint of our genetic potential, influencing our physical traits, health predispositions, and even aspects of our cognitive abilities. Similarly, our career path is influenced by our unique strengths, talents, and interests. In this essay, we will explore the intriguing relationship between career paths and DNA, examining how our genetic makeup can shape our professional journey and the ways in which understanding our DNA can empower us to make informed decisions about our career choices.

The Influence of DNA on Career Path

Our DNA plays a significant role in shaping various aspects of our lives, including our career paths. Genetic factors can influence our natural abilities, predispositions, and cognitive traits, which can ultimately impact our career choices and performance. For example, certain genetic variations have been associated with enhanced cognitive abilities in specific domains, such as analytical thinking or creative problem-solving. Individuals with these genetic predispositions may find themselves naturally inclined toward careers that require those particular skills, such as scientific research, engineering, or artistic pursuits.

Moreover, our DNA can influence our personality traits, which can play a crucial role in determining our career preferences and job satisfaction. Introversion and extraversion, for instance, have been linked to genetic factors. Introverts may thrive in careers that allow for independent work and deeper introspection, such as writing, research, or programming. On the other hand, extroverts may be drawn to careers that involve frequent social interactions and teamwork, such as sales, marketing, or public relations.

Additionally, our genetic makeup can impact our physical attributes and health, which can indirectly influence career choices. For instance, individuals with genetic predispositions for athleticism or physical coordination may find themselves naturally inclined toward careers in sports, fitness, or dance. Conversely, those with genetic predispositions for certain health conditions may feel motivated to pursue careers in healthcare or medical research, driven by a personal desire to make a difference and contribute to finding solutions.

DNA for Informed Career Choices

As our understanding of genetics continues to advance, individuals now have the opportunity to explore their DNA to gain insights into their unique strengths, talents, and potential career paths. DNA testing services, such as genetic profiling or genetic counseling, can provide individuals with information about their genetic predispositions, health risks, and ancestry. This knowledge can empower individuals to make more informed career choices based on their genetic makeup.

For example, a DNA analysis may reveal an individual's genetic predisposition for high levels of creativity. Armed with this knowledge, the individual may consider pursuing a career in the arts, design, or innovation, where their innate creative abilities can flourish. Similarly, a genetic profile that highlights exceptional problem-solving skills may guide an individual toward careers in technology, engineering, or scientific research.

Moreover, DNA testing can shed light on an individual's predisposition for certain health conditions. This information can be valuable in guiding career choices that align with personal values and aspirations. For instance, an individual with a genetic predisposition for cardiovascular diseases may choose a career in public health advocacy or medical research to contribute to the prevention and treatment of such conditions.

Informed by genetic insights, individuals can also make proactive choices regarding their personal and professional development. DNA analysis can provide information on how genetic variations may affect factors such as learning styles, memory retention, or adaptability to stress. Armed with this knowledge, individuals can tailor their learning strategies, seek appropriate training or educational opportunities, and create environments that support their unique genetic traits, ultimately enhancing their professional growth and success.

Ethical Considerations and Limitations

While the exploration of DNA and its influence on career paths is intriguing, it is essential to acknowledge the ethical considerations and limitations associated with this field. Genetic testing should always be approached with caution, ensuring privacy, informed consent, and responsible use of genetic information. Additionally, it is important to recognize that genetics is just one factor among many that contribute to an individual's career path. Environmental influences, personal experiences, education, and opportunities also play significant roles.

Furthermore, genetic information should not be seen as determinative of one's career choices or limitations. It is a tool that can provide insights and guidance, but ultimately, individuals have the capacity to shape their careers based on their interests, passions, and values. DNA analysis should be seen as a complement to self-reflection, career exploration, and guidance from professionals.

Although career paths and DNA may seem like distinct realms, they are interconnected in fascinating ways. Our genetic makeup influences our abilities, inclinations, and even our personality traits, which can shape our career choices and satisfaction. Understanding our DNA can empower us to make informed decisions about our career paths, capitalizing on our strengths and aligning our choices with our unique genetic predispositions. However, it is crucial to approach genetic insights with ethical considerations and recognize that genetics is just one piece of the puzzle. By embracing the synergies between DNA and career paths, individuals can navigate their professional journeys with greater self-awareness and purpose.

CHAPTER FOUR

The Power of College Education

Training and development play a pivotal role in career preparation, particularly within the context of colleges and universities. These institutions not only provide academic education but also have a responsibility to equip students with the necessary skills, knowledge, and competencies to thrive in their chosen careers. Together, we will explore the importance of training and development for career preparation in colleges and universities.

1. **Bridging the Gap between Education and Employment:** While formal education provides a foundation of theoretical knowledge, training and development programs bridge the gap between education and employment. They offer practical skills and industry-specific training that prepare students for the demands of the workforce. By offering relevant training, colleges and universities ensure that their graduates are well-equipped to meet the expectations and requirements of employers.

2. **Enhancing Employability:** Employers today seek candidates who possess a combination of academic qualifications and practical skills. Training and development programs within colleges and universities

focus on enhancing employability by providing students with industry-relevant skills. These programs help students develop specific competencies, such as communication, teamwork, problem-solving, and critical thinking, which are highly valued by employers.

3. **Keeping Pace with Industry Changes:** Industries are constantly evolving, driven by advancements in technology, changing market demands, and emerging trends. Training and development programs in colleges and universities enable students to stay updated with these changes. They provide opportunities to learn about the latest industry practices, tools, and technologies, ensuring that graduates are prepared for the ever-changing professional landscape.

4. **Practical Application of Knowledge:** Training and development programs allow students to apply the theoretical knowledge gained in classrooms to real-world scenarios. They provide hands-on experiences, simulations, case studies, and internships that enable students to practice and refine their skills in a practical setting. This practical application enhances their understanding, confidence, and problem-solving abilities, making them more prepared for their future careers.

5. **Networking and Professional Connections:** Training and development programs often provide opportunities for students to network with professionals, industry experts, and alumni. These connections can be invaluable in terms of mentorship, job opportunities, and access to industry insights. Building a strong professional network during college can significantly enhance career prospects and open doors to new possibilities.

6. **Lifelong Learning:** Training and development programs instill a culture of lifelong learning in students. They emphasize the importance of continuous skill development and encourage individuals to stay updated with industry trends. By nurturing a mindset of lifelong learning, colleges and universities prepare students to adapt to changing job requirements, embrace new technologies, and take on new challenges throughout their careers.

7. **Personal and Professional Growth:** Training and development programs contribute to the holistic growth of students. They not only focus on developing technical skills but also emphasize personal and professional development. These programs often include modules on leadership, communication, time management, and emotional intelligence, enabling students to

become well-rounded individuals capable of success in their careers and personal lives.

Training and development are vital components of career preparation within colleges and universities. By offering practical skills, enhancing employability, keeping pace with industry changes, facilitating the application of knowledge, fostering networking opportunities, promoting lifelong learning, and supporting personal and professional growth, training and development programs ensure that students are well-prepared to embark on successful careers upon graduation.

Higher Education and Economic Well-being

Higher education plays a vital role in human growth, development, and the overall well-being of individuals and society as a whole. It is a transformative phase of learning that equips individuals with knowledge, skills, and critical thinking abilities necessary to navigate the complexities of the modern world. Together, we will explore the significance of higher education in promoting human growth and development, as well as its impact on economic and financial well-being.

1. **Acquisition of Knowledge and Intellectual Development:** Higher education serves as a gateway to acquiring specialized knowledge and intellectual development. It provides opportunities for in-depth study in various fields, enabling individuals to gain expertise

in their chosen areas of interest. Through rigorous academic programs, individuals are exposed to diverse perspectives, theories, and research, fostering critical thinking, analytical skills, and problem-solving abilities. This intellectual growth enhances personal development and equips individuals with the tools to contribute meaningfully to society.

2. **Personal and Professional Development:** Higher education promotes personal and professional development by offering a comprehensive range of academic programs, extracurricular activities, and opportunities for self-exploration. Students have the chance to explore their passions, interests, and talents, thereby discovering their strengths and areas of specialization. Furthermore, higher education institutions provide a supportive environment for personal growth, nurturing essential skills such as communication, teamwork, leadership, and adaptability. These skills are invaluable in both professional and personal contexts, contributing to overall growth and well-being.

3. **Social and Cultural Awareness:** Higher education fosters social and cultural awareness by exposing individuals to a diverse range of perspectives, ideas, and cultures. Through interactions with

classmates, faculty, and the broader university community, students develop a broader worldview, tolerance, and empathy. Exposure to different cultures, languages, and traditions cultivates a sense of inclusivity and respect for diversity. These experiences prepare individuals to navigate a globalized world, fostering intercultural competence and promoting harmony in a multicultural society.

4. **Promotion of Critical Thinking and Research Skills:** Higher education encourages the development of critical thinking and research skills, which are essential for personal growth and societal progress. Students are encouraged to question, analyze, and evaluate information critically, enabling them to make informed decisions and challenge existing paradigms. The research-focused nature of higher education nurtures curiosity, innovation, and problem-solving abilities. These skills are invaluable in the workforce, where individuals are required to adapt to complex and ever-changing environments.

5. **Economic and Financial Well-being:** Higher education plays a significant role in driving economic and financial well-being at both individual and societal levels. Graduates with higher education qualifications tend to have higher earning potentials and better job

prospects compared to those with lower educational attainment. Higher education equips individuals with specialized skills that are in demand in the labor market, making them more competitive and sought after by employers. Additionally, higher education contributes to technological advancements, innovation, and productivity, which are key drivers of economic growth and prosperity.

6. **Social Mobility and Equality:** Higher education serves as a powerful tool for social mobility and reducing socioeconomic inequalities. It provides opportunities for individuals from diverse backgrounds to access quality education and improve their life circumstances. By leveling the playing field and providing equal educational opportunities, higher education promotes social justice, equal access to resources, and the empowerment of marginalized communities. It acts as a catalyst for social change, breaking the cycle of poverty and creating a more equitable society.

7. **Contribution to Research, Innovation, and Knowledge Creation:** Higher education institutions are the engines of research, innovation, and knowledge creation. Through academic research, scholars and students generate new ideas, insights, and discoveries that contribute to advancements in various fields. Higher education

institutions serve as hubs for collaboration between academia, industry, and government, fostering innovation and technological advancements. This research-driven environment not only benefits the academic community but also has far-reaching societal impacts, driving economic growth, and addressing pressing global challenges.

8. **Civic Engagement and Community Development:** Higher education encourages civic engagement and community development by instilling a sense of social responsibility in individuals. Universities often promote volunteerism, community service, and social outreach programs, encouraging students to actively contribute to their communities. This engagement enhances empathy, social awareness, and leadership skills, preparing individuals to become active and responsible citizens. Higher education institutions also serve as intellectual hubs that provide expertise and resources to address local and global challenges, driving positive social change.

Higher education is of paramount significance in promoting human growth, development, and economic well-being. It provides opportunities for the acquisition of knowledge, intellectual and personal development, social and cultural awareness, critical thinking, and research skills. Higher education not only contributes to individual growth but also plays a crucial role in driving economic prosperity, social mobility, equality, and community development. It equips individuals with the tools to navigate an increasingly complex world, fosters innovation and research, and prepares individuals to become active participants in society. The impact of higher education extends far beyond the individual, creating a better future for individuals, communities, and society as a whole.

CHPATER FIVE

Careers by Profession

In today's competitive job market, choosing a professional career that aligns with your skills, interests, and educational background is crucial for long-term success and job satisfaction. The world offers a wide range of career options across various disciplines, each with its own unique demands, opportunities, and rewards. In this book, we will explore professional careers by discipline, highlighting some of the key fields and the potential pathways to success within them.

It's important to note that these are just a few examples of professional careers within different disciplines. Within each discipline, there are numerous specializations and opportunities for growth and advancement. When choosing a career path, it's important to consider your interests, strengths, values, and long-term goals. Conducting research, seeking guidance from career counselors, and gaining practical experience through internships or part-time jobs can help you make informed decisions. Remember that success in any profession requires continuous learning, adaptability, and a passion for what you do.

Evolving job market, individuals are faced with a plethora of career options across various disciplines. Choosing a professional career that aligns with one's interests, skills, and educational background is crucial for long-term success and personal fulfillment. This essay aims to provide a comprehensive analysis of professional careers by discipline, highlighting the key fields and pathways to success within each discipline. By understanding the diverse opportunities available, individuals can make informed decisions about their career paths.

Professional careers span across various disciplines, each offering unique opportunities, challenges, and rewards. Choosing the right career path requires careful consideration of one's interests, skills, educational background, and long-term goals. The analysis provided in this essay highlights the diverse range of professional careers available in engineering and technology, healthcare and medicine, business and finance, creative arts and design, education and teaching, legal and criminal justice, social sciences and humanities, environmental and sustainability, communication and media, and technology and IT disciplines. By exploring these disciplines and understanding the pathways to success within each, individuals can make informed decisions about their career choices and embark on fulfilling and rewarding professional journeys.

Careers in Social Sciences

The field of social sciences encompasses a broad range of disciplines that study human society, behavior, and interactions. Careers in social sciences offer individuals the opportunity to explore and understand various aspects of the social world, and make meaningful contributions to society. Together, we will examine some of the careers within the social sciences and discuss their benefits.

1. **Sociologist:** Sociology is the study of social behavior, institutions, and societies. Sociologists examine social trends, conduct research, and analyze issues such as inequality, social change, and group dynamics. Sociologists play a vital role in understanding and addressing complex social problems, such as poverty, discrimination, and crime. They often work in research organizations, universities, government agencies, or non-profit organizations. The benefits of a career in sociology include the opportunity to contribute to social change, enhance social policy, and gain a deeper understanding of human behavior and societal structures.

2. **Anthropologist:** Anthropology is the study of human societies and cultures. Anthropologists explore various aspects of human life, including language, beliefs, kinship systems, and social structures. They conduct fieldwork, analyze data, and contribute to our understanding of diverse cultures around the world. Anthropologists often work in academia, museums, cultural resource management firms, or international

development organizations. A career in anthropology offers the chance to immerse oneself in different cultures, promote cultural understanding, and address contemporary issues such as cultural heritage preservation, human rights, and indigenous rights.

3. **Political Scientist:** Political science focuses on the study of political systems, institutions, and behavior. Political scientists analyze the distribution of power, decision-making processes, and political ideologies. They may specialize in areas such as international relations, comparative politics, or public policy. Political scientists often work in government agencies, think tanks, universities, or as consultants. The benefits of a career in political science include the opportunity to influence public policy, engage in diplomatic relations, and contribute to the democratic process.

4. **Psychologist:** Psychology is the scientific study of the mind and behavior. Psychologists explore various aspects of human cognition, emotions, and personality. They apply their knowledge to understand individual and group behavior, assess mental health, and develop therapeutic interventions. Psychologists work in a variety of settings, including hospitals, clinics, schools, research institutions, and private practice. A career in psychology offers the chance to help

individuals overcome challenges, promote mental well-being, and contribute to the advancement of psychological knowledge.

5. **Economist:** Economics is the study of how societies allocate scarce resources to satisfy human needs and wants. Economists analyze economic systems, market behavior, and the impact of policies on economic outcomes. They work in a wide range of sectors, including government agencies, financial institutions, research organizations, and international organizations. The benefits of a career in economics include the opportunity to influence economic policies, conduct economic research, and contribute to the understanding of global economic trends.

6. **Geographer:** Geography explores the relationship between humans and their environment. Geographers study spatial patterns, landforms, climate, and human activities across the globe. They analyze geographic data, conduct fieldwork, and contribute to urban planning, environmental conservation, or transportation planning. Geographers work in government agencies, research institutions, consulting firms, or non-profit organizations. A career in geography offers the chance to address pressing environmental issues, understand the impact of human activities on the planet, and contribute to sustainable development.

7. **Social Worker:** Social work focuses on helping individuals, families, and communities overcome challenges and improve their well-being. Social workers provide counseling, advocacy, and support services to vulnerable populations, such as children, the elderly, or individuals experiencing homelessness. They work in various settings, including hospitals, schools, social service agencies, and non-profit organizations. The benefits of a career in social work include the opportunity to make a positive impact on people's lives, advocate for social justice, and address systemic inequalities.

These are just a few examples of the many careers available within the social sciences. Each field offers its unique benefits, including the opportunity to contribute to society, address social issues, conduct research, and gain a deeper understanding of human behavior and societal dynamics. Careers in social sciences are intellectually stimulating, socially meaningful, and have the potential to create positive change in the world. If you have a passion for understanding human society and behavior, a career in social sciences may be a fulfilling and rewarding path to consider.

Careers in Physical Sciences

The field of physical sciences encompasses disciplines that focus on understanding the fundamental principles that govern the natural world. It explores the laws of physics, chemistry, astronomy, and earth sciences. Careers in physical sciences offer individuals the opportunity to engage in scientific research, exploration, and innovation. Together, we will examine some of the careers within the physical sciences and discuss their benefits.

1. **Physicist:** Physics is the study of matter, energy, and the fundamental forces of the universe. Physicists explore the laws that govern the behavior of atoms, and the cosmos. They conduct experiments, develop theories, and apply their knowledge to various fields such as engineering, technology, and medicine. Physicists work in academia, research institutions, government laboratories, and industries. The benefits of a career in physics include the opportunity to contribute to cutting-edge research, advance technological innovations, and unravel the mysteries of the universe.

2. **Chemist:** Chemistry focuses on the properties, composition, and transformations of matter. Chemists study the structure of molecules, chemical reactions, and the synthesis of new compounds. They work in

research and development, quality control, forensic science, and environmental analysis. Chemists play a crucial role in various industries, including pharmaceuticals, materials science, and energy. The benefits of a career in chemistry include the opportunity to develop new materials, contribute to advancements in medicine, and address environmental challenges.

3. **Geoscientist:** Geoscience encompasses the study of the Earth, its structure, processes, and history. Geoscientists examine topics such as geology, meteorology, oceanography, and environmental science. They conduct fieldwork, analyze data, and contribute to our understanding of the Earth's past, present, and future. Geoscientists work in academia, government agencies, energy companies, and environmental consulting firms. The benefits of a career in geoscience include the opportunity to explore the Earth's mysteries, contribute to sustainable resource management, and address pressing environmental issues such as climate change and natural disasters.

4. **Astronomer:** Astronomy is the study of celestial objects, including stars, planets, galaxies, and the universe as a whole. Astronomers observe and analyze the motion, composition, and behavior of celestial bodies. They work in observatories,

research institutions, and space agencies. Astronomers contribute to our understanding of the cosmos, uncover the origins of the universe, and search for signs of extraterrestrial life. The benefits of a career in astronomy include the opportunity to make groundbreaking discoveries, engage in space exploration missions, and inspire the public's curiosity about the universe.

5. **Materials Scientist:** Materials science focuses on the study of the properties, structure, and applications of materials. Materials scientists develop and analyze new materials with desirable properties for various industries, including electronics, energy, and healthcare. They work in research laboratories, manufacturing companies, and academic institutions. A career in materials science offers the chance to contribute to technological advancements, develop sustainable materials, and revolutionize industries.

6. **Environmental Scientist:** Environmental science examines the impact of human activities on the environment and seeks sustainable solutions to environmental challenges. Environmental scientists study ecosystems, natural resources, pollution, and climate change. They work in government agencies, non-profit organizations, consulting firms, and research institutions.

The benefits of a career in environmental science include the opportunity to protect and conserve the natural environment, promote sustainable practices, and influence environmental policy.

7. **Meteorologist:** Meteorology is the study of weather patterns, climate, and the atmosphere. Meteorologists observe and analyze weather conditions, forecast weather events, and study climate change. They work in weather forecasting agencies, research institutions, media outlets, and aviation companies. A career in meteorology offers the opportunity to contribute to weather prediction, mitigate the impacts of severe weather events, and understand the complexities of Earth's climate system.

These are just a few examples of the many careers available within the physical sciences. Each field offers its unique benefits, including the opportunity to engage in scientific exploration, contribute to technological advancements, and address global challenges. Careers in physical sciences are intellectually stimulating, offer opportunities for discovery and innovation, and have the potential to create a positive impact on society. If you have a passion for understanding the natural world and a curiosity about how it works, a career in physical sciences may be a fulfilling and rewarding path to consider.

Careers in Business

The field of business encompasses a wide range of industries and disciplines, offering individuals diverse career opportunities. Business careers involve various aspects of management, finance, marketing, entrepreneurship, and more. Together, we will explore some of the careers in business and discuss their benefits.

1. **Business Manager:** Business managers oversee the operations and overall performance of an organization. They are responsible for setting strategic goals, managing resources, and making decisions that drive business growth. Business managers work in a variety of industries, including finance, healthcare, retail, and technology. The benefits of a career in business management include the opportunity to lead teams, make a significant impact on organizational success, and develop a broad set of skills that are transferable across industries.

2. **Financial Analyst:** Financial analysts assess investment opportunities, analyze financial data, and provide recommendations to individuals or organizations. They work in banks, investment firms, and corporations, helping clients make informed decisions about investments, mergers and acquisitions, or financial planning. The benefits of a career

in financial analysis include the opportunity to work in a dynamic and challenging field, help clients achieve their financial goals, and build expertise in financial markets.

3. **Marketing Manager:** Marketing managers develop and implement strategies to promote products or services, increase brand awareness, and attract customers. They conduct market research, analyze consumer behavior, and oversee advertising campaigns. Marketing managers work in various industries, including consumer goods, technology, and entertainment. The benefits of a career in marketing management include the opportunity to be creative, shape consumer perceptions, and drive business growth through effective marketing strategies.

4. **Entrepreneur:** Entrepreneurs are individuals who start their own businesses or ventures. They identify opportunities, develop innovative ideas, and take calculated risks to build successful enterprises. Entrepreneurs can work in any industry or sector, creating their own path and driving their own success. The benefits of a career as an entrepreneur include the opportunity to pursue one's passion, have autonomy and control over business decisions, and potentially achieve financial rewards.

5. **Human Resources Manager:** Human resources (HR) managers are responsible for managing an organization's human capital. They oversee recruitment, employee training and development, compensation and benefits, and employee relations. HR managers work in various industries, ensuring that the organization has a skilled and motivated workforce. The benefits of a career in human resources management include the opportunity to work with people, shape organizational culture, and contribute to the professional growth and well-being of employees.

6. **Operations Manager:** Operations managers are responsible for overseeing the day-to-day operations of a business. They ensure that resources are allocated efficiently, processes are streamlined, and quality standards are met. Operations managers work in manufacturing companies, logistics firms, and service-oriented organizations. The benefits of a career in operations management include the opportunity to improve operational efficiency, solve complex problems, and contribute to overall organizational success.

7. **Sales Manager:** Sales managers lead sales teams and are responsible for achieving revenue targets and building relationships with clients. They develop sales strategies,

train sales representatives, and monitor sales performance. Sales managers work in various industries, such as retail, pharmaceuticals, or technology. The benefits of a career in sales management include the opportunity to drive revenue growth, build strong professional networks, and be rewarded for achieving sales targets.

8. **Supply Chain Manager:** Supply chain managers oversee the movement of goods and services from suppliers to customers. They manage logistics, inventory, and relationships with suppliers and distributors. Supply chain managers work in manufacturing companies, retail organizations, and logistics firms. The benefits of a career in supply chain management include the opportunity to optimize processes, ensure timely delivery of products, and contribute to cost savings for the organization.

9. **Management Consultant:** Management consultants provide expert advice to organizations to improve their performance and solve business problems. They analyze operations, develop strategies, and implement changes to enhance efficiency and profitability. Management consultants work for consulting firms or as independent consultants, serving clients across industries. The benefits of a career in management

consulting include the opportunity to work on diverse projects, tackle complex challenges, and provide valuable insights and recommendations to clients.

10. **Business Analyst:** Business analysts analyze business processes, identify areas for improvement, and develop solutions to enhance efficiency and profitability. They work closely with stakeholders, gather requirements, and translate them into actionable plans. Business analysts work in various industries and may be employed by consulting firms, technology companies, or within organizations. The benefits of a career in business analysis include the opportunity to work with cross-functional teams, bridge the gap between business and technology, and drive process improvements.

These are just a few examples of the many careers available within the field of business. Each career offers its unique benefits, including the opportunity to have a significant impact on organizations, work in dynamic and evolving industries, and develop a wide range of skills that are valuable in the business world. If you have an interest in business, a career in this field can provide you with exciting opportunities for growth, professional development, and success.

Careers in Accounting and Finance

The fields of accounting and finance offer a wide range of career opportunities for individuals interested in working with numbers, analyzing financial data, and making strategic financial decisions. These professions are crucial to the success and stability of organizations across industries. Together, we will explore some of the careers in accounting and finance and discuss their benefits.

1. **Accountant:** Accountants play a vital role in managing and analyzing financial information for organizations. They prepare financial statements, track expenses and revenues, and ensure compliance with financial regulations. Accountants work in various settings, including public accounting firms, corporations, non-profit organizations, and government agencies. The benefits of a career in accounting include job stability, strong earning potential, and opportunities for professional growth. Accountants also develop skills in financial analysis, problem-solving, and attention to detail.

2. **Financial Analyst:** Financial analysts assess investment opportunities, analyze financial data, and provide recommendations to individuals or organizations. They work in banks, investment firms, and corporations, helping clients make informed decisions

about investments, mergers and acquisitions, or financial planning. The benefits of a career in financial analysis include the opportunity to work in a dynamic and challenging field, help clients achieve their financial goals, and build expertise in financial markets. Financial analysts also develop strong analytical and communication skills.

3. **Auditor:** Auditors examine financial records, assess internal controls, and ensure compliance with regulations and standards. They work in public accounting firms, corporations, and government agencies. Auditors play a crucial role in providing independent assessments of financial statements and helping organizations identify and mitigate financial risks. The benefits of a career in auditing include the opportunity to work with a variety of clients, gain a deep understanding of financial operations, and contribute to the integrity and transparency of financial reporting.

4. **Financial Manager:** Financial managers are responsible for the overall financial health of an organization. They develop financial strategies, manage budgets, and make investment decisions. Financial managers work in various industries, such as banking, healthcare, or manufacturing. The benefits of a career in financial management include the opportunity to have a significant impact on

organizational performance, work closely with senior management, and play a key role in strategic decision-making. Financial managers also enjoy competitive salaries and potential for career advancement.

5. **Tax Consultant:** Tax consultants assist individuals and organizations in understanding and complying with tax laws. They provide advice on tax planning, prepare tax returns, and help clients optimize their tax positions. Tax consultants work in public accounting firms, tax advisory firms, or as independent consultants. The benefits of a career in tax consulting include the opportunity to work with diverse clients, keep up with changing tax regulations, and provide valuable tax strategies and solutions.

6. **Risk Manager:** Risk managers assess and manage financial risks faced by organizations. They identify potential risks, develop risk management strategies, and implement measures to mitigate risks. Risk managers work in various industries, including insurance, banking, and corporate risk management departments. The benefits of a career in risk management include the opportunity to protect organizations from financial losses, contribute to strategic decision-making, and ensure business continuity in the face of uncertainties.

7. **Investment Banker:** Investment bankers facilitate capital raising, mergers and acquisitions, and other financial transactions for corporations and institutions. They provide financial advice, structure deals, and help clients navigate complex financial transactions. Investment bankers work in investment banks, financial advisory firms, or in-house corporate finance departments. The benefits of a career in investment banking include the opportunity to work on high-profile deals, interact with senior executives, and enjoy lucrative compensation packages. Investment bankers also develop strong analytical, negotiation, and communication skills.

8. **Financial Planner:** Financial planners assist individuals in managing their personal finances, setting financial goals, and developing strategies to achieve those goals. They provide advice on investment planning, retirement planning, and risk management. Financial planners can work in financial planning firms, banks, or as independent consultants. The benefits of a career in financial planning include the opportunity to make a positive impact on individuals' financial well-being, build long-term relationships with clients, and provide holistic financial advice.

9. **Treasury Analyst:** Treasury analysts manage an organization's cash flow, liquidity, and financial investments. They analyze financial markets, monitor cash positions, and make recommendations for optimizing cash management. Treasury analysts work in corporations, financial institutions, and treasury management departments. The benefits of a career in treasury analysis include the opportunity to work with complex financial instruments, ensure liquidity for organizations, and contribute to financial decision-making.

10. **Corporate Finance Analyst:** Corporate finance analysts work within organizations to analyze financial data, evaluate investment opportunities, and support strategic decision-making. They assess the financial viability of projects, conduct financial modeling, and provide recommendations on capital allocation. Corporate finance analysts work in corporations, consulting firms, or financial advisory departments. The benefits of a career in corporate finance analysis include the opportunity to work directly with senior management, contribute to the organization's growth and profitability, and develop strong financial analysis and communication skills.

These are just a few examples of the many careers available within the fields of accounting and finance. Each career offers its unique benefits, including opportunities for professional growth, job stability, competitive salaries, and the ability to make a significant impact on organizations' financial health and success. If you have an aptitude for numbers, analytical thinking, and a passion for financial management, a career in accounting and finance can be a rewarding and fulfilling choice.

Careers in Healthcare

The field of healthcare offers a vast range of rewarding and fulfilling career opportunities for individuals interested in making a positive impact on people's lives. From direct patient care to research and administration, healthcare careers provide opportunities to contribute to the well-being of individuals, communities, and society as a whole. Together, we will explore some of the careers in healthcare and discuss their benefits.

1. **Physician:** Physicians, also known as doctors or medical doctors, diagnose and treat illnesses and injuries. They work in various medical specialties, such as family medicine, internal medicine, surgery, pediatrics, and many others. Physicians provide direct patient care, prescribe medications, order diagnostic tests, and perform procedures. The benefits of a career as a physician include the opportunity to save lives, improve health outcomes, and build meaningful relationships with patients. Physicians also enjoy intellectual

stimulation, ongoing learning, and competitive salaries.

2. **Nurse:** Nurses play a crucial role in patient care and are the backbone of healthcare delivery. They provide direct patient care, administer medications, monitor patients' conditions, and educate individuals and families about health management. Nurses work in various settings, including hospitals, clinics, long-term care facilities, and home healthcare. The benefits of a career in nursing include the opportunity to provide hands-on care, advocate for patients, and make a positive impact on their well-being. Nursing offers a wide range of specialties and flexible career paths.

3. **Medical Laboratory Scientist:** Medical laboratory scientists, also known as medical technologists, perform laboratory tests to aid in the diagnosis and treatment of diseases. They analyze samples, operate sophisticated laboratory equipment, and interpret results. Medical laboratory scientists work in hospitals, research laboratories, and diagnostic centers. The benefits of a career as a medical laboratory scientist include the opportunity to contribute to accurate diagnoses, conduct research, and play a crucial role in patient care. This field offers a combination of laboratory work, scientific exploration, and critical thinking.

4. **Pharmacist:** Pharmacists are experts in medications. They dispense prescription medications, educate patients on proper medication use, and collaborate with healthcare providers to ensure safe and effective drug therapies. Pharmacists work in community pharmacies, hospitals, research institutions, and pharmaceutical companies. The benefits of a career as a pharmacist include the opportunity to improve patients' health outcomes, prevent medication errors, and play a critical role in healthcare teams. Pharmacists also enjoy a high level of job stability and competitive salaries.

5. **Physical Therapist:** Physical therapists help individuals recover from injuries and improve their physical function. They assess patients' conditions, develop personalized treatment plans, and guide patients through exercises and therapies. Physical therapists work in hospitals, rehabilitation centers, private practices, and sports clinics. The benefits of a career as a physical therapist include the opportunity to improve patients' quality of life, promote mobility and independence, and witness the progress of patients' recovery. Physical therapists also enjoy a high level of job satisfaction and the chance to work with diverse patient populations.

6. **Occupational Therapist:** Occupational therapists assist individuals in regaining and developing skills necessary for daily activities and work. They help patients with physical, developmental, or cognitive disabilities overcome barriers and maximize their functional abilities. Occupational therapists work in hospitals, rehabilitation centers, schools, and mental health facilities. The benefits of a career as an occupational therapist include the opportunity to make a positive impact on individuals' lives, promote independence, and facilitate meaningful participation in daily activities. Occupational therapists also enjoy a high level of job satisfaction and the ability to work with diverse populations.

7. **Medical Researcher:** Medical researchers contribute to scientific advancements and improve healthcare outcomes through research. They design and conduct studies, analyze data, and publish findings. Medical researchers work in academic institutions, research organizations, pharmaceutical companies, and government agencies. The benefits of a career as a medical researcher include the opportunity to advance scientific knowledge, develop new treatments and interventions, and contribute to the overall improvement of healthcare. Medical researchers also enjoy intellectual stimulation, collaboration with experts in the

field, and the potential for making groundbreaking discoveries.

8. **Healthcare Administrator:** Healthcare administrators manage healthcare facilities, oversee operations, and ensure efficient delivery of healthcare services. They handle budgets, develop policies and procedures, and coordinate various departments within healthcare organizations. Healthcare administrators work in hospitals, clinics, nursing homes, and government agencies. The benefits of a career in healthcare administration include the opportunity to make a positive impact on healthcare systems, improve patient care delivery, and drive organizational success. Healthcare administrators also enjoy a combination of managerial responsibilities and the chance to contribute to strategic decision-making.

9. **Mental Health Counselor:** Mental health counselors provide support and therapy to individuals struggling with mental health issues, emotional challenges, and life transitions. They assess clients' needs, develop treatment plans, and offer guidance and counseling. Mental health counselors work in private practices, mental health clinics, schools, and community centers. The benefits of a career as a mental health counselor include the opportunity to help individuals overcome mental health

challenges, provide emotional support, and promote overall well-being. Mental health counselors also enjoy the satisfaction of seeing clients improve their mental health and lead fulfilling lives.

10. **Health Educator:** Health educators promote wellness and educate individuals and communities about healthy lifestyles, disease prevention, and health management. They develop educational materials, conduct workshops and presentations, and advocate for healthy behaviors. Health educators work in healthcare organizations, community centers, schools, and government agencies. The benefits of a career as a health educator include the opportunity to make a positive impact on public health, empower individuals to make informed decisions about their health, and promote healthy communities. Health educators also enjoy the satisfaction of seeing positive changes in individuals' behaviors and attitudes towards health.

These are just a few examples of the many careers available within the healthcare field. Each career offers its unique benefits, including the opportunity to make a difference in people's lives, job stability, opportunities for professional growth, and the satisfaction of contributing to the well-being of individuals and communities. If you have a passion for helping others, a strong desire to make a positive impact on healthcare, and an interest in scientific and medical knowledge, a career in healthcare may be a fulfilling and rewarding choice.

Careers in Journalism

Journalism is a dynamic and influential field that plays a crucial role in shaping public opinion, promoting transparency, and delivering accurate information to society. Journalists are responsible for gathering, analyzing, and presenting news and stories across various media platforms. A career in journalism offers numerous benefits for individuals passionate about storytelling, investigation, and the pursuit of truth. Together, we will explore some of the careers in journalism and discuss their benefits.

1. **News Reporter:** News reporters work on the front lines of journalism, covering local, national, or international news stories. They research, interview sources, and write books or produce news segments. News reporters work for newspapers, magazines, television stations, radio stations, and online media outlets. The benefits of a career as a news reporter include the opportunity to inform the public, uncover important stories, and contribute to the free flow of information. News reporters also enjoy the thrill of working on breaking news stories and the chance to travel and experience diverse cultures and events.

2. **Investigative Journalist:** Investigative journalists examine deep into issues, uncover hidden truths, and expose corruption, misconduct, or wrongdoing. They research, interview sources, analyze data, and write in-depth investigative reports. Investigative journalists work for media organizations or operate as independent journalists. The benefits of a career as an investigative journalist include the opportunity to hold powerful entities accountable, effect social change, and shed light on important issues. Investigative journalists also enjoy the satisfaction of making a significant impact on society through their work.

3. **Broadcast Journalist:** Broadcast journalists deliver news and stories through television or radio broadcasts. They report live from the field, anchor news programs, conduct interviews, and present stories to the audience. Broadcast journalists work for television networks, radio stations, and online broadcasting platforms. The benefits of a career as a broadcast journalist include the opportunity to reach a large audience, engage with viewers or listeners, and deliver news in real-time. Broadcast journalists also enjoy the excitement of working in a fast-paced environment and the chance to develop strong on-camera or on-air presentation skills.

4. **Photojournalist:** Photojournalists tell stories through compelling images. They capture photographs that accompany news books or standalone photo books. Photojournalists work for newspapers, magazines, wire services, and online media outlets. The benefits of a career as a photojournalist include the ability to capture impactful moments, evoke emotions through visual storytelling, and document important events or social issues. Photojournalists also enjoy the opportunity to travel, experience different cultures, and contribute to visual storytelling in the media.

5. **Feature Writer:** Feature writers focus on in-depth, human-interest stories that go beyond the news headlines. They conduct interviews, research topics, and write engaging, longer-form books. Feature writers work for newspapers, magazines, online publications, and freelance for various media outlets. The benefits of a career as a feature writer include the opportunity to explore diverse subjects, examine personal narratives, and provide in-depth analysis. Feature writers also enjoy the freedom to showcase their writing style and creativity while delivering thought-provoking and compelling stories.

6. **Editorial Writer:** Editorial writers' express opinions and provide commentary on current events or social issues. They write editorials

or opinion pieces for newspapers, magazines, or online platforms. Editorial writers aim to persuade, inform, or provoke discussions on important topics. The benefits of a career as an editorial writer include the opportunity to contribute to public discourse, shape public opinion, and advocate for social change. Editorial writers also enjoy the freedom to express their viewpoints and engage in critical analysis and commentary.

7. **Foreign Correspondent:** Foreign correspondents report on international news stories from different regions around the world. They provide on-the-ground coverage, conduct interviews, and report on political, social, and cultural developments. Foreign correspondents work for media organizations with global coverage. The benefits of a career as a foreign correspondent include the opportunity to travel, experience different cultures, and report on global issues. Foreign correspondents also enjoy the challenge of adapting to new environments and the chance to provide unique perspectives on international events.

8. **News Producer:** News producers oversee the creation and coordination of news programs or segments. They develop story ideas, manage production teams, and ensure the smooth execution of news broadcasts.

News producers work for television networks, radio stations, or online media outlets. The benefits of a career as a news producer include the opportunity to shape news content, make editorial decisions, and oversee the production process. News producers also enjoy the challenge of working in a fast-paced, collaborative environment and the chance to create engaging and informative news programs.

9. **Multimedia Journalist:** Multimedia journalists utilize a combination of skills, such as writing, reporting, videography, and editing, to deliver news stories across various platforms. They create content for print, online, television, and social media. Multimedia journalists work for media organizations or operate as independent journalists. The benefits of a career as a multimedia journalist include the opportunity to adapt to changing media landscapes, tell stories using different mediums, and engage with diverse audiences. Multimedia journalists also enjoy the creative freedom and the ability to learn and utilize various multimedia tools and technologies.

10. **News Anchor:** News anchors serve as the face of news programs, delivering news stories and providing commentary. They present news in a professional and engaging manner, often with a team of reporters and

correspondents. News anchors work for television networks, radio stations, or online media outlets. The benefits of a career as a news anchor include the opportunity to connect with the audience, deliver information with authority, and provide context to news stories. News anchors also enjoy the chance to build a recognizable on-air presence and develop strong communication skills.

These are just a few examples of the many careers available within the field of journalism. Each career offers its unique benefits, including the opportunity to inform, educate, and engage with the public, contribute to social change, and provide a voice to the voiceless. If you have a passion for storytelling, a desire to uncover the truth, and a dedication to upholding the principles of journalism, a career in journalism may be a fulfilling and impactful choice.

Careers in Religion

Religion plays a significant role in the lives of many individuals and communities around the world. It provides spiritual guidance, fosters a sense of community, and offers a framework for understanding life's meaning and purpose. For those with a deep interest in religious studies and a desire to serve others, a career in religion can be rewarding and fulfilling. Together, we will explore some of the careers in religion and discuss their benefits.

1. **Clergy:** Clergy members, such as priests, pastors, imams, rabbis, or religious leaders, serve as spiritual guides for their respective religious communities. They conduct religious services, lead worship, provide pastoral care, and offer counseling and support to their congregations. The benefits of a career as clergy include the opportunity to make a positive impact on individuals' spiritual lives, provide guidance and comfort during challenging times, and foster a sense of belonging within a religious community. Clergy members also have the satisfaction of living out their faith and serving others in a meaningful way.

2. **Religious Educator:** Religious educators teach and educate others about religious traditions, beliefs, and practices. They work in educational institutions, such as religious schools, seminaries, universities, or community centers. Religious educators develop curriculum, lead classes, facilitate discussions, and provide guidance on religious matters. The benefits of a career as a religious educator include the opportunity to share knowledge and wisdom, shape religious understanding and awareness, and inspire others to explore their faith. Religious educators also have the chance to foster critical thinking and promote interfaith dialogue and understanding.

3. **Chaplain:** Chaplains offer spiritual and emotional support to individuals in various settings, such as hospitals, prisons, military organizations, or universities. They provide comfort, guidance, and counseling to those in need, irrespective of their religious affiliation. The benefits of a career as a chaplain include the opportunity to bring solace and hope to individuals facing challenging circumstances, provide moral and ethical guidance, and be a compassionate presence in times of crisis. Chaplains also enjoy the diversity of working with people from different backgrounds and the chance to make a positive impact on their lives.

4. **Religious Writer/Journalist:** Religious writers and journalists focus on producing content related to religious topics, spirituality, or religious news. They write books, books, or blog posts, or work for media organizations to cover religious stories. The benefits of a career as a religious writer or journalist include the opportunity to explore and express one's own faith or engage with various religious traditions, promote religious understanding and dialogue, and inform the public about religious matters. Religious writers and journalists also enjoy the freedom of expression and the ability to contribute to the public discourse on religion.

5. **Religious Counselor/Therapist:** Religious counselors or therapists integrate religious beliefs and principles into their counseling or therapeutic practices. They provide guidance, support, and mental health services to individuals or couples based on their religious worldview. The benefits of a career as a religious counselor or therapist include the opportunity to address individuals' spiritual and emotional needs, help them navigate religious challenges, and integrate faith into their healing process. Religious counselors and therapists also have the chance to combine their passion for psychology or counseling with their religious beliefs.

6. **Religious Nonprofit Administrator:** Religious nonprofit administrators oversee the operations and management of religious-based organizations, such as charities, community centers, or advocacy groups. They handle budgeting, fundraising, program development, and staff management. The benefits of a career as a religious nonprofit administrator include the opportunity to make a positive impact on social issues aligned with religious values, organize and lead community initiatives, and create a sense of belonging and support for individuals in need. Religious nonprofit administrators also enjoy the satisfaction of contributing to the

welfare of others and promoting social justice.

7. **Academic Scholar of Religion:** Academic scholars of religion engage in research and teaching about various aspects of religious traditions, including their history, beliefs, practices, and cultural impact. They work in universities, colleges, or research institutions. The benefits of a career as an academic scholar of religion include the opportunity to deepen one's understanding of religious traditions, contribute to academic discourse, and mentor the next generation of religious scholars. Academic scholars of religion also have the freedom to pursue their research interests and engage in intellectual debates.

8. **Interfaith Coordinator:** Interfaith coordinators facilitate dialogue, understanding, and cooperation among individuals from different religious backgrounds. They organize interfaith events, promote interfaith initiatives, and foster respect and appreciation for religious diversity. Interfaith coordinators work in religious organizations, educational institutions, or interfaith organizations. The benefits of a career as an interfaith coordinator include the opportunity to build bridges between religious communities, promote religious tolerance and cooperation, and create spaces for dialogue and

collaboration. Interfaith coordinators also enjoy the satisfaction of fostering understanding and harmony among people of different faiths.

9. **Religious Artist:** Religious artists use their creative talents, such as painting, sculpture, music, or literature, to express religious themes or ideas. They create art that inspires, uplifts, and reflects religious beliefs and experiences. The benefits of a career as a religious artist include the opportunity to express one's faith through artistic expression, evoke emotions and contemplation in viewers or listeners, and contribute to the spiritual and aesthetic enrichment of others. Religious artists also enjoy the freedom to explore religious symbolism and create works that convey spiritual messages.

10. **Missionary/Religious Worker:** Missionaries or religious workers dedicate themselves to spreading their religious beliefs and values to communities around the world. They engage in community development, humanitarian work, or evangelism, depending on their specific religious calling. The benefits of a career as a missionary or religious worker include the opportunity to make a direct impact on people's lives, promote positive change, and serve marginalized communities.

Missionaries and religious workers also gain valuable cultural experiences, build cross-cultural relationships, and deepen their own faith through their service.

These are just a few examples of the many careers available within the field of religion. Each career offers its unique benefits, including the opportunity to make a meaningful difference in people's lives, explore and express one's own faith, foster spiritual growth and understanding, and contribute to the well-being of individuals and communities. If you have a deep interest in religious studies, a passion for spiritual matters, and a desire to serve others, a career in religion may be a fulfilling and impactful choice.

Careers in Philosophy

Philosophy is the study of fundamental questions about existence, knowledge, ethics, and the nature of reality. It is a field that encourages critical thinking, intellectual exploration, and the pursuit of wisdom. While some may perceive philosophy as an abstract discipline, it offers a wide range of rewarding careers that can have a significant impact on individuals and society. Together, we will explore some of the careers in philosophy and discuss their benefits.

1. **Philosophy Professor:** Philosophy professors teach philosophy courses at colleges and universities. They engage in research, publish academic papers, and mentor students. The benefits of a career as a

philosophy professor include the opportunity to share knowledge, inspire critical thinking, and shape the minds of future generations. Philosophy professors also enjoy the freedom to explore philosophical concepts, engage in intellectual discussions, and contribute to the development of philosophical ideas.

2. **Ethicist:** Ethicists specialize in studying ethical principles, moral reasoning, and ethical decision-making. They work in various settings, including academic institutions, think tanks, corporations, or government agencies. Ethicists analyze complex moral dilemmas, provide guidance on ethical issues, and develop ethical frameworks. The benefits of a career as an ethicist include the opportunity to influence ethical policies, promote ethical behavior, and contribute to the development of a more just and compassionate society. Ethicists also enjoy the intellectual challenge of grappling with ethical questions and applying philosophical principles to real-world situations.

3. **Policy Analyst:** Policy analysts utilize their philosophical training to analyze and evaluate public policies. They work in government agencies, think tanks, or advocacy organizations. Policy analysts assess the ethical, social, and philosophical implications of policies and provide

recommendations for improvement. The benefits of a career as a policy analyst include the opportunity to shape public policy, advocate for social justice, and contribute to the betterment of society. Policy analysts also enjoy the intellectual stimulation of analyzing complex issues and the chance to make a practical impact through policy change.

4. **Writer/Author:** Writers and authors with a background in philosophy explore philosophical ideas through their writing. They produce philosophical books, books, books, or opinion pieces. The benefits of a career as a writer/author in philosophy include the opportunity to share philosophical insights with a wider audience, provoke thought and introspection, and contribute to public discourse. Writers and authors also enjoy the creative freedom to express philosophical ideas in engaging and accessible ways.

5. **Consultant:** Philosophy consultants offer their expertise in critical thinking, logic, and ethical reasoning to help individuals, organizations, or businesses address complex problems. They provide guidance on ethical decision-making, analyze arguments, and facilitate philosophical discussions. The benefits of a career as a philosophy consultant include the opportunity to apply

philosophical thinking to practical situations, offer valuable insights, and assist clients in making informed choices. Philosophy consultants also enjoy the variety of working with different clients and industries.

6. **Researcher:** Philosophical researchers explore specific areas of philosophy in-depth through academic research. They investigate philosophical concepts, theories, or historical developments and contribute to the advancement of philosophical knowledge. The benefits of a career as a philosophical researcher include the opportunity to examine philosophical questions, challenge existing assumptions, and make original contributions to the field. Researchers also enjoy the intellectual freedom to pursue their interests and engage in scholarly dialogue.

7. **Mediator:** Mediators use their philosophical skills to facilitate dialogue and resolve conflicts. They help parties in dispute find common ground, understand different perspectives, and reach mutually acceptable solutions. Mediators work in various contexts, including legal settings, community organizations, or international diplomacy. The benefits of a career as a mediator with a background in philosophy include the opportunity to promote understanding and reconciliation, foster peaceful resolutions, and improve communication. Mediators also

enjoy the satisfaction of facilitating positive outcomes and helping individuals or groups find common ground.

8. **Journalist:** Journalists with a background in philosophy apply critical thinking and analytical skills to reporting on complex issues. They investigate and analyze social, political, or ethical topics, providing informed and thoughtful perspectives. The benefits of a career as a journalist in philosophy include the opportunity to inform the public, hold power to account, and contribute to public debate. Journalists also enjoy the dynamic nature of the profession and the chance to engage with a wide range of subjects and ideas.

9. **Curator/Museum Educator:** Curators and museum educators with a background in philosophy work in art, history, or cultural institutions. They develop exhibitions, interpret artifacts, and engage visitors in philosophical discussions related to the exhibits. The benefits of a career as a curator or museum educator in philosophy include the opportunity to promote philosophical reflection through cultural artifacts, encourage critical thinking, and enhance visitors' understanding of art and culture. Curators and museum educators also enjoy the creativity involved in designing exhibits

and the chance to make philosophy accessible and engaging to diverse audiences.

10. **Social Entrepreneur:** Social entrepreneurs with a background in philosophy combine their passion for social change with innovative business models. They create enterprises or organizations that address social, environmental, or ethical challenges. The benefits of a career as a social entrepreneur in philosophy include the opportunity to make a positive impact, promote social justice, and address pressing societal issues. Social entrepreneurs also enjoy the autonomy and creativity involved in developing solutions and the chance to integrate philosophical principles into their ventures.

These are just a few examples of the many careers available within the field of philosophy. Each career offers its unique benefits, including the opportunity to engage in intellectual exploration, promote critical thinking, contribute to ethical decision-making, and make a positive impact on individuals and society. If you have a passion for deep thinking, questioning assumptions, and exploring life's big questions, a career in philosophy may be a rewarding and fulfilling choice.

Careers in Social Work

Social work is a profession dedicated to promoting social change, enhancing well-being, and improving the lives of individuals, families, and communities. Social workers work in various settings, such as hospitals, schools, nonprofit organizations, government agencies, and community centers. They provide support, advocacy, and resources to those in need. Together, we will explore some of the careers in social work and discuss their benefits.

1. **Clinical Social Worker:** Clinical social workers provide mental health services to individuals, families, and groups. They assess clients' needs, develop treatment plans, and provide therapy to address emotional, behavioral, and psychological challenges. The benefits of a career as a clinical social worker include the opportunity to make a positive impact on clients' mental health and well-being, promote personal growth, and facilitate healing. Clinical social workers also enjoy the deep connections they form with clients and the satisfaction of witnessing positive change.

2. **Child and Family Social Worker:** Child and family social workers focus on supporting children and families in need. They may work in child protection agencies, adoption agencies, or family support organizations. Child and family social

workers assess family situations, provide counseling and support, and ensure the safety and well-being of children. The benefits of a career as a child and family social worker include the opportunity to protect vulnerable children, strengthen family relationships, and help families overcome challenges. Child and family social workers also enjoy the satisfaction of advocating for children's rights and contributing to their overall well-being.

3. **School Social Worker:** School social workers play a crucial role in supporting students' academic success and emotional well-being. They work in educational settings, collaborating with students, parents, and teachers. School social workers provide counseling, develop intervention plans, and connect students and families with community resources. The benefits of a career as a school social worker include the opportunity to make a positive impact on students' lives, promote inclusivity and social justice within the education system, and contribute to a nurturing and supportive school environment. School social workers also enjoy the variety of working with diverse student populations and the satisfaction of helping students overcome obstacles.

4. **Medical and Healthcare Social Worker:** Medical and healthcare social workers work in hospitals, clinics, or other healthcare settings. They provide support and resources to patients and their families, helping them navigate the healthcare system and cope with medical conditions. Medical social workers assist with discharge planning, coordinate care services, and provide emotional support. The benefits of a career as a medical and healthcare social worker include the opportunity to make a difference in patients' lives, provide holistic care, and advocate for patients' rights and well-being. Medical social workers also enjoy the interdisciplinary nature of their work, collaborating with healthcare professionals to ensure patients receive comprehensive support.

5. **Community Social Worker:** Community social workers focus on improving the well-being of entire communities. They work with community organizations, grassroots initiatives, or government agencies to identify community needs, develop programs, and advocate for social change. Community social workers address issues such as poverty, homelessness, substance abuse, and access to resources. The benefits of a career as a community social worker include the opportunity to work towards social justice, empower communities, and

create sustainable change. Community social workers also enjoy the collaborative nature of their work and the ability to engage with diverse populations.

6. **Geriatric Social Worker:** Geriatric social workers specialize in supporting older adults and their families. They may work in nursing homes, assisted living facilities, or home care agencies. Geriatric social workers assess the needs of older adults, coordinate care services, and provide emotional support. They also assist families in navigating complex healthcare and long-term care systems. The benefits of a career as a geriatric social worker include the opportunity to improve the quality of life for older adults, promote healthy aging, and ensure older adults have access to appropriate resources and support. Geriatric social workers also enjoy the meaningful connections they form with older adults and their families.

7. **Crisis Intervention Specialist:** Crisis intervention specialists provide immediate support and resources to individuals experiencing a crisis situation, such as survivors of trauma, domestic violence, or natural disasters. They work in crisis hotlines, emergency shelters, or community response teams. Crisis intervention specialists offer emotional support, safety planning, and referrals to necessary services.

The benefits of a career as a crisis intervention specialist include the opportunity to provide immediate assistance to individuals in distress, offer a lifeline during difficult times, and help individuals navigate through crises towards healing and resilience. Crisis intervention specialists also enjoy the dynamic nature of their work and the ability to make an immediate impact on people's lives.

8. **Policy Advocate:** Policy advocates work at the intersection of social work and policy. They analyze social issues, propose policy solutions, and advocate for change at the local, national, or international level. Policy advocates collaborate with lawmakers, community organizations, and other stakeholders to influence legislation and create social change. The benefits of a career as a policy advocate include the opportunity to address systemic issues, promote social justice, and advocate for marginalized populations. Policy advocates also enjoy the opportunity to shape policies and create lasting impact on a larger scale.

9. **Researcher/Evaluator:** Researchers and evaluators in social work contribute to the field's knowledge base by conducting research studies and program evaluations. They collect and analyze data to assess the effectiveness of social interventions, develop

evidence-based practices, and inform policy decisions. The benefits of a career as a social work researcher or evaluator include the opportunity to contribute to the advancement of the profession, improve the effectiveness of social programs, and drive evidence-based practice. Researchers and evaluators also enjoy the intellectual stimulation of conducting research and the ability to influence social work practice at a broader level.

10. **Private Practice Social Worker:** Private practice social workers have their own independent practices and offer counseling, therapy, or other social work services directly to clients. They have the flexibility to choose their client populations, set their own schedules, and tailor their practice to their areas of expertise. The benefits of a career as a private practice social worker include the autonomy and independence of running a business, the ability to develop deep and long-lasting therapeutic relationships with clients, and the opportunity to create a practice that aligns with personal values and goals.

These are just a few examples of the many careers available in social work. Each career offers its unique benefits, including the opportunity to make a positive impact on individuals and communities, promote social justice, and improve the overall well-being of society. If you have a passion for helping others, a commitment to social justice, and a desire to make a meaningful difference in people's lives, a career in social work may be a fulfilling and rewarding choice.

Careers in Mathematics

Mathematics is a fundamental discipline that plays a critical role in various fields, including science, technology, finance, and engineering. A career in mathematics offers numerous benefits, including intellectual stimulation, problem-solving opportunities, and the ability to make a significant impact in a wide range of industries. Together, we will explore some of the careers in mathematics and discuss their benefits.

1. **Mathematician:** Mathematicians engage in theoretical research and apply mathematical principles to solve complex problems. They develop new mathematical theories, algorithms, and models to address real-world challenges. The benefits of a career as a mathematician include the opportunity to contribute to the advancement of mathematical knowledge, solve intellectually stimulating problems, and make groundbreaking discoveries. Mathematicians also enjoy the interdisciplinary nature of their work, collaborating with scientists, engineers, and researchers in other fields.

2. **Data Scientist:** Data scientists utilize mathematical and statistical techniques to extract insights from large datasets. They analyze data, develop models, and provide data-driven solutions to business problems. Data scientists work in various industries, including technology, finance, healthcare, and marketing. The benefits of a career as a data scientist include the opportunity to work with cutting-edge technology, make data-driven decisions, and contribute to innovation. Data scientists also enjoy the high demand for their skills and the potential for lucrative career opportunities.

3. **Actuary:** Actuaries use mathematical and statistical methods to assess and manage risk in the insurance and finance industries. They analyze data, evaluate probabilities, and develop models to determine insurance premiums, investment strategies, and pension plans. The benefits of a career as an actuary include the opportunity to work in a stable and well-compensated profession, use mathematical skills to make financial predictions, and help individuals and organizations make informed decisions. Actuaries also enjoy the ability to apply mathematical principles to real-world scenarios and the potential for professional growth.

4. **Financial Analyst:** Financial analysts utilize mathematical and statistical techniques to evaluate investment opportunities, assess financial performance, and make recommendations for financial decision-making. They work in banking, investment firms, or corporate finance departments. The benefits of a career as a financial analyst include the opportunity to work in the dynamic field of finance, apply quantitative skills to analyze market trends, and contribute to informed investment strategies. Financial analysts also enjoy the potential for high earning potential and the ability to make a tangible impact on financial outcomes.

5. **Operations Research Analyst:** Operations research analysts use mathematical and analytical techniques to optimize business operations and solve complex logistical problems. They apply mathematical modeling, simulation, and optimization methods to improve efficiency and decision-making in areas such as supply chain management, transportation, and production. The benefits of a career as an operations research analyst include the opportunity to solve real-world problems, enhance organizational efficiency, and drive cost savings. Operations research analysts also enjoy the interdisciplinary nature of their work, collaborating with professionals in various fields.

6. **Statistician:** Statisticians collect, analyze, and interpret data to extract meaningful insights and support decision-making. They design experiments, develop survey methodologies, and apply statistical techniques to draw conclusions from data. Statisticians work in various industries, including healthcare, government, market research, and academia. The benefits of a career as a statistician include the opportunity to work with data, identify trends and patterns, and provide evidence-based solutions. Statisticians also enjoy the versatility of their skills, as statistical analysis is relevant in virtually all fields.

7. **Cryptographer:** Cryptographers use mathematical algorithms and techniques to secure information and develop cryptographic systems. They work in areas such as computer science, cybersecurity, and national security. Cryptographers design encryption algorithms, analyze their security, and develop strategies to protect sensitive data. The benefits of a career as a cryptographer include the opportunity to contribute to information security, combat cyber threats, and develop innovative cryptographic solutions. Cryptographers also enjoy the intellectual challenge of developing complex algorithms and the potential to work on high-impact projects.

8. **Researcher:** Mathematics researchers work in academia or research institutions, exploring new mathematical theories, solving open problems, and publishing their findings. They contribute to the development of mathematics as a discipline and collaborate with other researchers to advance knowledge. The benefits of a career as a mathematics researcher include the opportunity to pursue one's passion for mathematics, work on cutting-edge projects, and make significant contributions to mathematical knowledge. Researchers also enjoy the freedom to explore new ideas and the prestige associated with academic achievements.

9. **Mathematical Modeller:** Mathematical modellers apply mathematical techniques to create models that represent complex systems, such as climate patterns, population dynamics, or economic trends. They use mathematical modeling software and simulations to understand and predict the behavior of these systems. The benefits of a career as a mathematical modeller include the opportunity to work on interdisciplinary projects, contribute to solving real-world problems, and provide valuable insights to inform decision-making. Mathematical modellers also enjoy the creativity involved in developing models and the ability to apply

mathematical principles to a wide range of domains.

10. **Mathematics Educator:** Mathematics educators teach and inspire students at various levels, from primary school to university. They develop curriculum, design instructional materials, and engage students in mathematical learning. The benefits of a career as a mathematics educator include the opportunity to make a difference in students' lives, foster critical thinking and problem-solving skills, and contribute to shaping future generations. Mathematics educators also enjoy the satisfaction of seeing students grasp mathematical concepts and the potential for mentorship and academic leadership.

These are just a few examples of the many careers available in mathematics. Each career offers its unique benefits, including the opportunity to apply mathematical skills to real-world problems, engage in intellectually stimulating work, and make a significant impact in various industries. If you have a passion for mathematics, logical reasoning, and problem-solving, a career in mathematics may provide you with a rewarding and fulfilling professional journey.

Careers in Politics and Government

Careers in politics and government offer individuals the opportunity to shape public policy, serve their communities, and make a positive impact on society. Working in these fields involves engaging in the democratic process, advocating for change, and addressing pressing issues at local, national, or international levels. Together, we will explore some of the careers in politics and government and discuss their benefits.

1. **Politician/Elected Official:** Politicians and elected officials hold public office and represent their constituents' interests and concerns. They develop policies, pass legislation, and make decisions that impact the lives of individuals and communities. The benefits of a career as a politician or elected official include the opportunity to influence public policy, address social issues, and advocate for positive change. Politicians also enjoy the ability to engage with diverse communities, build coalitions, and lead transformative initiatives.

2. **Government Administrator:** Government administrators work in various departments and agencies, overseeing operations, implementing policies, and managing resources. They ensure that government programs and services are delivered effectively and efficiently. The benefits of a

career as a government administrator include the opportunity to shape policy implementation, improve public service delivery, and contribute to good governance. Government administrators also enjoy the potential for career advancement and the ability to work on a broad range of issues.

3. **Diplomat:** Diplomats represent their countries in international relations, promoting diplomacy, negotiating agreements, and resolving conflicts. They work in embassies, consulates, or international organizations. The benefits of a career as a diplomat include the opportunity to foster international cooperation, protect national interests, and contribute to global peace and stability. Diplomats also enjoy the cultural exchange and networking opportunities that come with working on an international stage.

4. **Policy Analyst:** Policy analysts work in government agencies, think tanks, or research organizations, conducting research, analyzing data, and providing evidence-based recommendations to policymakers. They assess the impact of policies, propose solutions to social issues, and contribute to the development of effective public policies. The benefits of a career as a policy analyst include the opportunity to influence decision-making, conduct in-depth research on

pressing issues, and contribute to positive social change. Policy analysts also enjoy the intellectual stimulation of analyzing complex problems and developing innovative solutions.

5. **Political Consultant:** Political consultants provide strategic advice and support to political campaigns, helping candidates connect with voters, shape their messages, and develop campaign strategies. They work in electoral campaigns, advocacy groups, or consulting firms. The benefits of a career as a political consultant include the opportunity to shape public opinion, influence electoral outcomes, and contribute to democratic processes. Political consultants also enjoy the fast-paced and dynamic nature of campaign work and the ability to work with a diverse range of clients.

6. **Legislative Aide:** Legislative aides work with elected officials in legislative bodies, providing research, writing, and administrative support. They assist in drafting legislation, analyzing bills, and coordinating constituent services. The benefits of a career as a legislative aide include the opportunity to contribute to the legislative process, work closely with policymakers, and engage with constituents on critical issues. Legislative aides also enjoy

the potential for career advancement within the political arena.

7. **Public Affairs Specialist:** Public affairs specialists work in government agencies, nonprofit organizations, or corporations, managing communication strategies, promoting public awareness, and engaging with the media. They develop messaging, coordinate public events, and respond to inquiries from the press and the public. The benefits of a career as a public affairs specialist include the opportunity to shape public opinion, build relationships with key stakeholders, and effectively communicate important messages. Public affairs specialists also enjoy the ability to work on diverse issues and navigate complex communication challenges.

8. **Political Researcher:** Political researchers work in academia, think tanks, or research organizations, conducting studies on political trends, public opinion, and electoral behavior. They analyze data, contribute to academic publications, and provide insights into political dynamics. The benefits of a career as a political researcher include the opportunity to advance knowledge in the field of political science, inform policy discussions, and contribute to evidence-based decision-making. Political researchers also enjoy the freedom to pursue independent

research and the potential for intellectual influence.

9. **Nonprofit Advocate:** Nonprofit advocates work for advocacy organizations, promoting social causes, influencing public opinion, and lobbying for policy change. They engage with legislators, community leaders, and the public to raise awareness about specific issues and drive social change. The benefits of a career as a nonprofit advocate include the opportunity to work for a cause one is passionate about, make a difference in the lives of vulnerable populations, and influence public policy. Nonprofit advocates also enjoy the ability to collaborate with like-minded individuals and build broad-based support for their cause.

10. **Public Servant:** Public servants work in various government agencies and departments, providing essential services to the public. They may be involved in areas such as education, healthcare, transportation, or environmental protection. The benefits of a career as a public servant include the opportunity to directly impact people's lives, contribute to the well-being of communities, and serve the public interest. Public servants also enjoy job security, competitive benefits, and the potential for professional growth within the public sector.

These are just a few examples of the many careers available in politics and government. Each career offers its unique benefits, including the opportunity to shape public policy, serve the community, and make a positive impact on society. If you have a passion for public service, a desire to engage in policy-making, and a commitment to improving the lives of others, a career in politics and government may provide you with a rewarding and fulfilling professional journey.

Careers in Higher Education

Higher education plays a vital role in society by fostering intellectual growth, expanding knowledge, and preparing individuals for professional careers. Careers in higher education offer individuals the opportunity to contribute to the academic community, engage in research and scholarship, and shape the minds of future generations. Together, we will explore some of the careers in higher education and discuss their benefits.

1. **Professor:** Professors are at the forefront of higher education, teaching courses, conducting research, and mentoring students. They contribute to the knowledge base in their respective fields through scholarly publications and research projects. The benefits of a career as a professor include the opportunity to share knowledge, inspire students, and engage in groundbreaking research. Professors also enjoy the autonomy

and intellectual freedom associated with pursuing their research interests.

2. **Academic Advisor:** Academic advisors guide students in their academic journeys, helping them navigate degree requirements, select courses, and explore career pathways. They provide guidance, support, and resources to help students make informed decisions about their educational and career goals. The benefits of a career as an academic advisor include the opportunity to make a positive impact on students' lives, foster their personal and academic growth, and help them succeed in their chosen fields. Academic advisors also enjoy the fulfillment of seeing students achieve their educational aspirations.

3. **Researcher:** Researchers in higher education institutions contribute to advancing knowledge and understanding in various fields. They conduct research projects, secure funding, publish findings in scholarly journals, and collaborate with other researchers. The benefits of a career as a researcher include the opportunity to examine deep into specific areas of interest, contribute to academic discourse, and make significant discoveries. Researchers also enjoy the intellectual stimulation and the potential for professional recognition within their academic communities.

4. **Librarian:** Librarians in higher education institutions manage library resources, provide research assistance, and promote information literacy. They help students and faculty navigate through vast databases, access relevant information, and conduct effective research. The benefits of a career as a librarian include the opportunity to support the learning and research needs of students and faculty, promote access to knowledge, and contribute to the scholarly community. Librarians also enjoy the dynamic nature of their work and the ability to stay at the forefront of information resources and technologies.

5. **Academic Administrator:** Academic administrators work in various administrative roles within higher education institutions, such as department chairs, deans, or provosts. They oversee academic programs, manage budgets, and provide leadership and direction to faculty and staff. The benefits of a career as an academic administrator include the opportunity to shape academic policies, foster institutional growth, and contribute to the strategic vision of the institution. Academic administrators also enjoy the potential for career advancement and the ability to influence the direction of academic programs.

6. **Career Counselor:** Career counselors in higher education institutions help students explore career options, develop job search strategies, and navigate the transition from academia to the workforce. They provide guidance on career planning, resume building, and networking. The benefits of a career as a career counselor include the opportunity to empower students in their career development, facilitate their transition to the professional world, and contribute to their long-term success. Career counselors also enjoy the satisfaction of seeing students secure meaningful employment.

7. **Institutional Researcher:** Institutional researchers gather and analyze data to inform decision-making and support institutional planning and assessment. They collect data on student enrollment, graduation rates, and other key metrics to help institutions evaluate their performance and improve student outcomes. The benefits of a career as an institutional researcher include the opportunity to contribute to data-informed decision-making, enhance institutional effectiveness, and support continuous improvement. Institutional researchers also enjoy working with diverse stakeholders and influencing institutional policies and practices.

8. **Admissions Officer:** Admissions officers are responsible for evaluating student applications, reviewing qualifications, and making admissions decisions. They play a crucial role in shaping the student body and ensuring a diverse and qualified student population. The benefits of a career as an admissions officer include the opportunity to identify talented and motivated students, contribute to the institutional reputation, and help shape the incoming class. Admissions officers also enjoy the satisfaction of witnessing students' educational journeys from application to graduation.

9. **Online Learning Specialist:** Online learning specialists design, develop, and deliver online courses and programs in higher education institutions. They leverage technology to create engaging and interactive learning experiences for remote students. The benefits of a career as an online learning specialist include the opportunity to expand access to education, embrace innovative teaching methods, and enhance the online learning environment. Online learning specialists also enjoy the flexibility and adaptability of online teaching and learning.

10. **Student Affairs Professional:** Student affairs professionals work in various roles, such as student services, residence life, or student activities. They support students'

personal and social development, provide resources and support systems, and create a positive campus environment. The benefits of a career as a student affairs professional include the opportunity to make a positive impact on students' lives outside the classroom, foster student engagement, and contribute to a vibrant campus community. Student affairs professionals also enjoy the satisfaction of seeing students thrive academically and personally.

These are just a few examples of the many careers available in higher education. Each career offers its unique benefits, including the opportunity to contribute to knowledge, shape students' lives, and advance in one's professional field. If you have a passion for education, a commitment to lifelong learning, and a desire to make a positive impact on students and the academic community, a career in higher education may provide you with a fulfilling and rewarding professional journey.

Careers in K-12

Careers in K-12 education are essential for nurturing young minds, providing quality education, and shaping the future of society. Working in K-12 education allows individuals to make a meaningful impact on students' lives, foster their intellectual and personal growth, and contribute to building a strong foundation for their future success. Together, we will explore some of the careers in K-12 education and discuss their benefits.

1. **Teacher:** Teachers are at the heart of K-12 education. They create lesson plans, deliver instruction, assess student progress, and provide support and guidance. Teachers have the opportunity to inspire a love of learning, instill knowledge and skills, and help students develop critical thinking and problem-solving abilities. The benefits of a career as a teacher include the opportunity to make a positive impact on students' lives, witness their growth and achievements, and contribute to shaping future generations. Teachers also enjoy the satisfaction of seeing students succeed academically and personally.

2. **School Administrator:** School administrators, such as principals and assistant principals, provide leadership and oversee the overall functioning of schools. They manage staff, develop policies, coordinate curriculum, and create a conducive learning environment. School administrators have the opportunity to shape the school's vision, improve educational outcomes, and foster a positive and inclusive school culture. The benefits of a career as a school administrator include the ability to influence educational practices, support

teacher development, and ensure a safe and effective learning environment for students.

3. **School Counselor:** School counselors play a crucial role in supporting students' social-emotional well-being and academic success. They provide guidance and counseling services, assist with academic planning, and address students' personal and social challenges. School counselors have the opportunity to make a positive impact on students' mental health, help them navigate life's challenges, and provide guidance in career exploration. The benefits of a career as a school counselor include the ability to create a supportive and nurturing environment, empower students to reach their full potential, and contribute to their overall well-being.

4. **Special Education Teacher:** Special education teachers work with students who have disabilities or special learning needs. They adapt curriculum, provide individualized instruction, and support students in developing their skills and reaching their academic goals. Special education teachers have the opportunity to make a significant difference in the lives of students with unique challenges, foster their inclusive participation in education, and advocate for their rights and needs. The benefits of a career as a special education

teacher include the ability to provide tailored support, witness students' progress and achievements, and promote inclusive education.

5. **School Librarian:** School librarians support students' information literacy skills, promote reading, and provide resources for learning. They curate collections, assist with research projects, and foster a love of reading among students. School librarians have the opportunity to cultivate a passion for lifelong learning, introduce students to diverse perspectives, and nurture their critical thinking abilities. The benefits of a career as a school librarian include the ability to promote literacy and knowledge acquisition, collaborate with teachers in integrating technology and information literacy, and create a vibrant learning environment.

6. **School Nurse:** School nurses provide medical care and support to students, ensuring their health and well-being during the school day. They administer medication, handle emergencies, and educate students about health-related topics. School nurses have the opportunity to promote preventive health practices, monitor students' health conditions, and contribute to a safe and healthy school environment. The benefits of a career as a school nurse include the ability to support students' physical and emotional

well-being, collaborate with parents and healthcare professionals, and address health-related barriers to learning.

7. **Curriculum Specialist/Instructional Coach:** Curriculum specialists or instructional coaches work with teachers to enhance instructional practices, develop curriculum, and facilitate professional development. They provide guidance and support to educators in implementing effective teaching strategies, incorporating new technologies, and aligning instruction with standards. Curriculum specialists/instructional coaches have the opportunity to improve instructional quality, promote innovation in teaching and learning, and support teachers' professional growth. The benefits of a career as a curriculum specialist/instructional coach include the ability to shape educational practices, collaborate with teachers in improving student outcomes, and foster a culture of continuous learning and improvement.

8. **School Psychologist:** School psychologists assess students' learning and behavioral needs, provide counseling services, and collaborate with teachers and parents to create supportive environments. They help identify and address learning disabilities, emotional challenges, and social issues that may impact students' academic progress.

School psychologists have the opportunity to support students' mental health, promote positive behavior, and contribute to creating inclusive and supportive learning environments. The benefits of a career as a school psychologist include the ability to make a difference in students' lives, collaborate with multidisciplinary teams, and advocate for students' well-being.

9. **Physical Education Teacher:** Physical education (PE) teachers promote physical fitness, healthy lifestyles, and motor skills development in students. They design and implement physical education programs, teach sports and exercise techniques, and encourage students to adopt active and healthy habits. PE teachers have the opportunity to promote lifelong physical fitness, instill values of teamwork and sportsmanship, and contribute to students' overall well-being. The benefits of a career as a PE teacher include the ability to combine education and physical activity, inspire students to lead healthy lives, and make a positive impact on their long-term health.

10. **Technology Integration Specialist:** Technology integration specialists work with teachers and students to integrate technology effectively into the learning process. They provide training, support, and guidance on using educational technologies, digital

resources, and online tools. Technology integration specialists have the opportunity to enhance teaching and learning through technology, promote digital literacy, and prepare students for a technologically advanced world. The benefits of a career as a technology integration specialist include the ability to foster innovation in education, empower teachers with technological skills, and help students develop critical digital competencies.

These are just a few examples of the many careers available in K-12 education. Each career offers its unique benefits, including the opportunity to shape young minds, foster educational growth, and make a lasting impact on students' lives. If you have a passion for education, enjoy working with children and adolescents, and have a desire to contribute to society by empowering future generations, a career in K-12 education may provide you with a fulfilling and rewarding professional journey.

Careers in Athletics

Athletics play a significant role in society, promoting physical fitness, teamwork, and personal development. Careers in athletics offer individuals the opportunity to combine their passion for sports with their professional aspirations. Whether as athletes, coaches, trainers, or sports administrators, these careers provide numerous benefits that go beyond the realm of competition. Together, we will explore some of the careers in athletics and discuss their benefits.

1. **Athlete:** Being an athlete is a dream for many sports enthusiasts. Athletes train rigorously to compete at the highest level in their chosen sport. The benefits of a career as an athlete include the opportunity to pursue a passion, showcase talent, and achieve personal and professional success. Athletes enjoy the thrill of competition, the satisfaction of pushing physical limits, and the potential for fame and recognition.

2. **Coach:** Coaches play a pivotal role in developing athletes' skills, strategies, and overall performance. They provide guidance, instruction, and motivation to help athletes reach their full potential. The benefits of a career as a coach include the opportunity to mentor and inspire athletes, shape their character, and contribute to their success on and off the field. Coaches also enjoy the satisfaction of seeing athletes develop their skills, achieve their goals, and grow as individuals.

3. **Athletic Trainer:** Athletic trainers are responsible for the health and well-being of athletes. They prevent, diagnose, and treat sports-related injuries, provide rehabilitation services, and educate athletes on injury prevention and proper conditioning. The

benefits of a career as an athletic trainer include the opportunity to support athletes' physical health, help them recover from injuries, and contribute to their overall performance and longevity. Athletic trainers also enjoy the satisfaction of playing a crucial role in athletes' well-being and success.

4. **Sports Administrator:** Sports administrators work behind the scenes to manage and coordinate various aspects of athletic programs. They handle logistics, finances, marketing, and operations to ensure the smooth functioning of sports organizations. The benefits of a career as a sports administrator include the opportunity to contribute to the overall development of athletic programs, shape policies, and create opportunities for athletes and fans. Sports administrators also enjoy the dynamic nature of their work and the ability to work in a fast-paced and exciting environment.

5. **Sports Agent:** Sports agents represent athletes and negotiate contracts, endorsements, and other business opportunities on their behalf. They help athletes secure lucrative deals, protect their interests, and navigate the complex world of sports business. The benefits of a career as a sports agent include the opportunity to work closely with athletes, build relationships with industry professionals, and contribute to their

clients' financial and professional success. Sports agents also enjoy the potential for financial rewards and the excitement of being involved in high-profile negotiations.

6. **Sports Journalist:** Sports journalists report on athletic events, provide analysis, and share stories about athletes and teams. They work in various media outlets, including print, broadcast, and digital platforms. The benefits of a career as a sports journalist include the opportunity to combine a passion for sports with storytelling, attend major sporting events, and interact with athletes and coaches. Sports journalists also enjoy the ability to shape public opinion, inform and entertain sports fans, and contribute to the sports media landscape.

7. **Sports Psychologist:** Sports psychologists work with athletes to enhance their mental and emotional well-being, optimize performance, and develop coping strategies for competition. They help athletes manage stress, build confidence, and improve focus and concentration. The benefits of a career as a sports psychologist include the opportunity to make a significant impact on athletes' mental health and performance, contribute to their overall well-being, and help them reach their full potential. Sports psychologists also enjoy the satisfaction of witnessing athletes' personal growth and resilience.

8. **Fitness Trainer/Strength and Conditioning Coach:** Fitness trainers and strength and conditioning coaches work with athletes to improve their physical fitness, strength, and conditioning. They develop training programs, provide guidance on nutrition, and monitor athletes' progress. The benefits of a career as a fitness trainer or strength and conditioning coach include the opportunity to promote health and fitness, work with athletes of all levels, and help them achieve their performance goals. Fitness trainers and strength and conditioning coaches also enjoy the satisfaction of seeing athletes make physical gains and excel in their respective sports.

9. **Sports Marketing Specialist:** Sports marketing specialists develop and implement marketing strategies for sports teams, organizations, or brands. They promote events, manage sponsorships, and engage fans through various marketing channels. The benefits of a career as a sports marketing specialist include the opportunity to combine a passion for sports with marketing expertise, create engaging campaigns, and connect with sports fans. Sports marketing specialists also enjoy the dynamic and exciting nature of the sports industry and the potential for career growth.

10. **Sports Event Planner:** Sports event planners coordinate and manage sporting events, such as tournaments, championships, or large-scale competitions. They handle logistics, venue arrangements, scheduling, and ensure the smooth execution of the event. The benefits of a career as a sports event planner include the opportunity to work on high-profile events, create memorable experiences for athletes and spectators, and contribute to the success of major sporting occasions. Sports event planners also enjoy the fast-paced and dynamic nature of their work and the satisfaction of seeing their plans come to life.

These are just a few examples of the many careers available in athletics. Each career offers its unique benefits, including the opportunity to work in a field one is passionate about, contribute to athletes' success and well-being, and be part of a vibrant and exciting industry. If you have a love for sports, a desire to make a positive impact in the athletic world, and a willingness to embrace challenges, a career in athletics may provide you with a fulfilling and rewarding professional journey.

CHAPTER SIX

The Narrative About Career Path

Once upon a time, in a world filled with endless career possibilities, individuals embarked on a journey to discover their professional paths. Each discipline held its own allure, captivating the hearts and minds of those who sought to make a difference and find fulfillment in their work. From the realms of engineering and technology to the realms of creative arts and design, the possibilities seemed boundless.

In the field of engineering and technology, individuals embraced the opportunity to create and innovate. They examined the world of mechanical engineering, designing marvels that propelled industries forward. They ventured into the realms of civil engineering, shaping cities and infrastructure with their expertise. In the field of computer science and information technology, individuals harnessed the power of algorithms and code, building software and networks that connected people around the globe. The field buzzed with excitement and endless possibilities, attracting those with a passion for problem-solving and a drive to shape the future.

Meanwhile, In the field of healthcare and medicine, individuals dedicated themselves to the noble pursuit of healing and caring for others. Doctors and nurses became beacons of hope, tending to the sick and wounded with compassion and skill. Medical researchers toiled diligently in laboratories, seeking breakthroughs that would revolutionize treatment and save lives. The field resonated with a sense of purpose and responsibility, drawing in those with a deep desire to make a tangible difference in the lives of others.

In the field of business and finance, individuals found themselves immersed in the world of numbers, strategy, and growth. They stepped into the shoes of entrepreneurs, braving the challenges of starting and scaling their own ventures. Others embraced the intricacies of accounting and finance, ensuring the financial health and stability of organizations. Marketing wizards crafted campaigns that captured the attention and hearts of consumers. The realm pulsed with energy and the promise of success, attracting those with a flair for leadership, a knack for numbers, and a hunger for success.

As the journey continued, individuals ventured into the realm of creative arts and design, where their imaginations knew no bounds. Graphic designers breathed life into visuals that told compelling stories. Fashion designers wove fabrics into wearable works of art. Architects sketched blueprints for structures that merged form and function. The world became a canvas, waiting to be painted with their creativity and vision. In this realm, individuals expressed their unique perspectives and added beauty to the world.

In the field of education and teaching, individuals embraced the opportunity to shape young minds and ignite a love for learning. They stepped into classrooms as educators, guiding students on a journey of knowledge and discovery. They became mentors, imparting wisdom and instilling values in the next generation. The realm resonated with the joy of seeing minds bloom and talents flourish, attracting those with a passion for nurturing and empowering others.

In the field of legal and criminal justice, individuals became guardians of justice and defenders of the law. Lawyers fought for the rights of the oppressed, ensuring justice prevailed. Law enforcement officers patrolled the streets, safeguarding communities and maintaining order. The realm resonated with a sense of duty and the pursuit of truth, drawing in those with a strong moral compass and a desire to protect and serve.

In the field of social sciences and humanities, individuals immersed themselves in the complexities of human behavior, society, and culture. Psychologists examined the depths of the human mind, seeking to understand the intricacies of thought and emotion. Sociologists studied the dynamics of communities and societies, unraveling the threads that bound them together. Historians unearthed stories of the past, illuminating the lessons that shaped the present. The realm buzzed with intellectual curiosity and the quest for knowledge, attracting those with a thirst for understanding and a passion for social change.

As the journey neared its end, individuals found themselves In the field of environmental and sustainability. Here, they embraced the responsibility of protecting and preserving the planet. Environmental scientists examined the intricacies of ecosystems, seeking to find harmony between human progress and ecological well-being. Conservationists fought to save endangered species and fragile habitats. The realm resonated with a call to action, drawing in those with a deep love for nature and a commitment to creating a sustainable future.

In the field of communication and media, individuals became storytellers and influencers. Journalists uncovered truths and brought them to light. Public relations professionals crafted narratives that shaped public perception. Digital media experts harnessed the power of technology to connect and engage. The realm resonated with the power of words and images, attracting those with a gift for storytelling and a passion for making their voices heard.

Finally, In the field of technology and IT, individuals examined the digital world, harnessing its power to transform industries and lives. Software developers created applications that simplified tasks and enhanced efficiency. Cybersecurity experts fortified digital fortresses, protecting sensitive information from malicious threats. Data analysts unraveled insights hidden within vast amounts of information. The realm hummed with the promise of innovation and progress, attracting those with a keen eye for technology and a drive to push boundaries.

And so, the journey through the realms of professional careers by discipline came to an end. Each realm offered its own unique challenges and rewards, attracting individuals with different passions, skills, and aspirations. Whether they found themselves drawn to the realms of engineering and technology, healthcare and medicine, business and finance, creative arts and design, education and teaching, legal and criminal justice, social sciences and humanities, environmental and sustainability, communication and media, or technology and IT, they embarked on a path that aligned with their interests, values, and talents.

In the vast tapestry of professional careers, individuals found their place, weaving their stories into the fabric of the world. Each discipline held the power to shape lives, communities, and the future. As they pursued their chosen paths, they discovered fulfillment, success, and a profound sense of purpose. And as the world evolved, new disciplines emerged, offering endless opportunities for those who dared to dream and embrace the ever-changing landscape of professional careers.

In this grand tapestry, individuals realized that their journeys were not just about choosing a career but about discovering their true selves. The disciplines they embraced reflected their passions, strengths, and the unique contributions they had to offer. As they ventured forth, they left their mark on the world, leaving a legacy that would inspire future generations to embark on their own journeys of self-discovery and professional success. And so, the interplay between professional careers and individual journeys continued, forever shaping the world and the lives of those who dared to dream and choose their own paths.

Do What You Are: Embracing Authenticity in Your Career

Authenticity is a powerful force that drives us to be true to ourselves, to embrace our unique qualities, and to pursue paths that align with our values and passions. In the field of career choices, the concept of "doing what you are" takes center stage, urging individuals to seek professional paths that resonate with their authentic selves. It is an approach that encourages individuals to discover their innate talents, interests, and personality traits and then leverage them to make informed career decisions. "Do what you are" is a mantra that promotes self-awareness, self-acceptance, and the pursuit of fulfillment and success on one's own terms.

At its core, "do what you are" emphasizes the importance of self-reflection and understanding. It encourages individuals to examine deep into their own psyche and uncover their true passions, talents, and motivations. This process involves introspection, self-assessment, and the exploration of one's values and beliefs. By gaining a deeper understanding of oneself, individuals can identify the career paths that align with their authentic selves, avoiding the trap of pursuing professions that don't resonate with who they truly are.

When we "do what we are," we tap into our natural strengths and talents. We embrace our unique abilities and leverage them to excel in our chosen fields. By aligning our work with our inherent skills and interests, we are more likely to experience a sense of flow, where our tasks feel effortless and rewarding. When we are in our element, work becomes less of a burden and more of a source of fulfillment and joy. We become more engaged, motivated, and productive, which in turn leads to greater success and satisfaction in our careers.

"Doing what you are" also means embracing authenticity in the workplace. It involves staying true to oneself, even in the face of societal expectations, trends, or external pressures. It means honoring our values, expressing our opinions, and standing up for what we believe in. Authenticity breeds trust, credibility, and meaningful connections with others. When we bring our genuine selves to the table, we contribute unique perspectives and ideas, fostering innovation and growth within our professional environments.

However, "doing what you are" does not imply a static or fixed career path. It recognizes that individuals are dynamic beings, capable of growth and change. Our authentic selves evolve over time, influenced by our experiences, learning, and personal development. Thus, "doing what you are" also encompasses the willingness to explore new interests, acquire new skills, and adapt to evolving circumstances. It encourages individuals to embrace opportunities for growth and to embrace career transitions that align with their evolving authentic selves.

To "do what you are," it is crucial to cultivate self-awareness and engage in continuous self-reflection. This can be achieved through various means, such as journaling, seeking feedback from trusted mentors or colleagues, and participating in self-assessment tools or career counseling sessions. The journey of self-discovery and aligning with our authentic selves is ongoing, requiring dedication, curiosity, and a willingness to challenge ourselves.

In a world where societal expectations, familial pressures, and cultural norms often shape our perceptions of success and happiness, "doing what you are" is a radical act of self-determination. It invites individuals to question conventional wisdom and define their own paths. It invites us to reject the notion that success is solely measured by external markers such as job titles or financial gains. Instead, it encourages us to prioritize personal fulfillment, passion, and a sense of purpose.

"Doing what you are" is a call to action. It challenges us to examine our lives and careers with a critical eye, asking ourselves if we are truly being authentic and aligned with our true selves. It invites us to take risks, pursue our passions, and make courageous choices that reflect our innermost desires. By doing so, we unlock the potential for a meaningful and fulfilling career—one that not only brings professional success but also enriches our lives on a profound level.

"Doing what you are" is a powerful mantra that urges individuals to embrace authenticity in their career choices. It encourages self-reflection, self-acceptance, and the pursuit of paths that align with our inherent talents, interests, and values. By following this principle, we unlock the potential for a fulfilling and successful career that is uniquely our own. So, let us dare to "do what we are" and embark on a journey of self-discovery and professional fulfillment.

ABOUT THE AUTHOR

Dr. Lester Reid is a distinguished expert in the fields of higher education, human development, training and development, business development, career coaching, executive coaching, accounting and finance, federal taxation, research and publication, education, facilitation, transformational speaking, transformational leadership, and an inspirational figure. With a wealth of knowledge and experience in these areas, Dr. Reid has made a significant impact on individuals, organizations, and communities through his expertise, guidance, and transformative approach.

In the field of higher education, Dr. Lester Reid is a recognized authority. He possesses extensive experience in academic settings, having served as a professor, mentor, and advisor to countless students. With a deep understanding of the challenges and opportunities faced by individuals pursuing higher education, Dr. Reid is dedicated to helping students navigate their academic journeys successfully. His expertise in career coaching and executive coaching allows him to provide invaluable guidance to students and professionals alike, helping them make informed decisions about their career paths and achieve their professional goals.

As a leader in the field of human development, Dr. Reid has devoted his career to empowering individuals to reach their full potential. He understands that personal growth and development are essential components of a fulfilling and successful life. Through his transformative approach, he helps individuals identify their strengths, overcome obstacles, and unlock their innate talents and abilities. Dr. Reid's expertise in training and development enables him to design and deliver impactful programs that inspire personal and professional growth.

Dr. Lester Reid's contributions to business development are noteworthy. He possesses a deep understanding of the intricacies of the business world, including finance, accounting, and taxation. With his expertise, he has guided businesses to achieve financial success, optimize their operations, and navigate complex tax regulations. Dr. Reid's ability to analyze data, identify opportunities, and implement strategic initiatives has made him an invaluable asset to organizations seeking growth and profitability.

Furthermore, to his professional expertise, Dr. Lester Reid is a renowned researcher and author. He has published numerous books and books on topics related to higher education, human development, business management, and transformational leadership. His research contributions have not only expanded the knowledge base in these fields but have also provided practical insights and guidance to professionals and academics alike. Dr. Reid's dedication to research and publication reflects his commitment to advancing the collective understanding of these critical areas of study.

As an educator and facilitator, Dr. Reid has touched the lives of many. His passion for teaching, combined with his ability to create engaging and transformative learning experiences, has inspired countless individuals to pursue their educational and personal goals. Dr. Reid's facilitation skills allow him to create safe and inclusive environments where individuals can explore new ideas, challenge their assumptions, and grow both intellectually and emotionally.

Perhaps one of Dr. Lester Reid's most remarkable qualities is his ability to inspire and motivate others through transformational speaking and leadership. He possesses the rare gift of connecting deeply with his audience, igniting a spark within them, and empowering them to pursue their dreams fearlessly. Dr. Reid's charisma, authenticity, and ability to convey complex ideas in a relatable manner make him a sought-after speaker and leader in various professional and personal development settings.

Dr. Lester Reid is an inspirational figure who has dedicated his life to higher education, human development, training and development, business development, career coaching, executive coaching, accounting and finance, federal taxation, research and publication, education, facilitation, transformational speaking, transformational leadership, and making a positive impact on the lives of others. Through his expertise, guidance, and transformative approach, he has helped individuals unlock their full potential, organizations achieve success, and communities thrive. Dr. Reid's contributions to these fields are invaluable, and his passion for empowering others serves as a beacon of inspiration to all who have the privilege of encountering his work.